WhatsApp's Global Domination

WhatsApp's Global Domination

Surge In Worldwide Users

Ehsan Sheroy

UNIEK ENTERPRISES

CONTENTS

INDEX 1

Chapter 1 3

Chapter 2 15

Chapter 3 27

Chapter 4 40

Chapter 5 54

Chapter 6 66

Chapter 7 78

Chapter 8 89

Chapter 9 100

INDEX

Chapter 1: Introduction
1.1 Overview of WhatsApp's rise to global prominence
1.2 Historical context of messaging platforms
1.3 Brief examination of early challenges and successes

Chapter 2: The Birth of WhatsApp
2.1 Background on the founders and their vision
2.2 The development and launch of the messaging platform
2.3 Initial reception and early user adoption

Chapter 3: Features and Evolution
3.1 In-depth exploration of WhatsApp's key features
3.2 The evolution of the platform over time
3.3 User feedback and how it shaped feature development

Chapter 4: User-Friendly Interface
4.1 Analysis of WhatsApp's user interface design
4.2 The role of simplicity in attracting a diverse user base
4.3 User experience and the platform's intuitive design

Chapter 5: Security and Privacy
5.1 Examination of WhatsApp's commitment to user privacy
5.2 Implementation of end-to-end encryption
5.3 Impact on user trust and global adoption

Chapter 6: Cultural Adaptability
6.1 WhatsApp's success in different linguistic and cultural contexts
6.2 Studies of its adoption in various regions

6.3 The role of language support and cultural sensitivity

Chapter 7: Strategic Integrations and Partnerships
7.1 Overview of WhatsApp's integration with Facebook-owned platforms
7.2 Analysis of strategic partnerships contributing to its global reach
7.3 The synergies that enhance user experience across platforms

Chapter 8: Surge in Emerging Markets
8.1 Exploration of WhatsApp's popularity in emerging economies
8.2 Factors contributing to its success in regions with diverse economic conditions
8.3 The platform's impact on communication trends in developing nations

Chapter 9: The Future of WhatsApp's Global Domination
9.1 Speculations on future developments and innovations
9.2 Potential challenges and opportunities for growth
9.3 WhatsApp's role in shaping the future of global digital communication

Chapter 1

Introduction

In the consistently developing scene of correspondence innovation, one stage has arisen as a worldwide peculiarity, reshaping the manner in which individuals associate and offer data across borders. WhatsApp, at first considered as a straightforward informing application, has gone through an extraordinary excursion since its beginning in 2009. What started as a modest startup established by Jan Koum and Brian Acton before long developed into a tech goliath that reformed the way people, organizations, and networks impart on a worldwide scale.

The ascent of WhatsApp can be credited to its easy to use point of interaction, unwavering quality, and obligation to client security. As cell phones became universal, WhatsApp immediately adjusted to the changing innovative scene, securing itself as the go-to informing application for millions around the world. The stage's prosperity lies in its consistent message informing as well as in its steady development, presenting highlights like voice messages, video calls, and start to finish encryption, which put it aside in a cutthroat market.

The worldwide reception of WhatsApp has been completely transient. Its client base extended quickly, rising above topographical limits and social contrasts. The application turned into an essential piece of day to day existence for individuals from varying backgrounds, giving a helpful and quick method for correspondence. From relaxed discussions to significant transactions, WhatsApp turned into the extension interfacing people and networks across the globe.

WhatsApp's excursion to worldwide mastery has been set apart by essential acquisitions and associations that supported its abilities and broadened its compass. Facebook's procurement of WhatsApp in 2014 for a faltering \$19 billion was a milestone second, flagging the developing significance of informing stages in the virtual entertainment scene. This securing infused significant assets into WhatsApp as well as prepared for combination with other Facebook-claimed administrations, further cementing its situation in the computerized biological system.

The stage's client base kept on taking off, powered by the presentation of new highlights and steady updates. WhatsApp's obligation to client protection, with start to finish encryption as a foundation, reverberated with clients looking for secure and confidential correspondence. In a time where information security concerns were at the front of public talk, WhatsApp's accentuation on safeguarding client data turned into a key differentiator.

As the world turned out to be more interconnected, WhatsApp adjusted to different phonetic and social requirements. The application's multilingual help and the capacity to associate clients from various language foundations added to its world-wide allure. From nearby organizations in developing business sectors to global enterprises, WhatsApp turned into a flexible apparatus for correspondence, rising above hindrances and working with culturally diverse trades.

The flood in overall clients was additionally determined by the stage's acknowledgment of the advancing idea of correspondence. With the coming of sight and sound rich substance, WhatsApp consolidated highlights like photograph and video sharing, making it an exhaustive correspondence center. The stage's easy to understand plan and natural elements made it available to people, everything being equal, further adding to its broad reception.

WhatsApp's effect stretched out past private correspondence, invading different parts of society. Organizations embraced the stage as an immediate and effective method for arriving at clients. The presentation of WhatsApp Business further worked with this pattern, giving endeavors instruments to draw in with their crowd, oversee client requests, and grandstand items or administrations. The harmonious connection among organizations and WhatsApp changed the stage into a unique commercial center.

The stage's impact was not restricted to created countries; it assumed a vital part in interfacing networks in arising economies where admittance to customary correspondence foundation was restricted. WhatsApp turned into a help for individuals in distant regions, empowering them to remain associated with the world and access data that was generally unattainable. This democratization of correspondence highlighted WhatsApp's importance in connecting advanced partitions and cultivating inclusivity.

Be that as it may, WhatsApp's excursion to worldwide mastery was not without challenges. The stage confronted examination in regards to security concerns and falsehood flowing on the stage. As the spread of bogus data turned into a major problem, WhatsApp went to proactive lengths to control the scattering of deluding content. The execution of highlights like message sending limits and instructive missions pointed toward advancing computerized education mirrored WhatsApp's obligation to alleviating these difficulties.

The stage's versatility notwithstanding affliction was apparent as it proceeded to improve and adjust. The presentation of the WhatsApp Pay include additionally extended its utility, permitting clients to make monetary exchanges consistently inside the application. This introduction to the monetary domain situated WhatsApp as a specialized instrument as well as a multi-layered stage taking care of different necessities.

Following worldwide occasions and outlook changes in the manner individuals work and impart, WhatsApp's job turned out to be significantly more articulated. The Coronavirus pandemic highlighted the significance of computerized correspondence, with WhatsApp filling in as a help for people and organizations wrestling with the difficulties of remote work and social separating. The stage's capacity to work with virtual associations and cooperative endeavors additionally set its pertinence in an advancing world.

As we dive into the unpredictable embroidery of WhatsApp's worldwide control, it becomes clear that its prosperity isn't simply a consequence of mechanical ability however a demonstration of how its might interpret human correspondence needs. The stage's development from a straightforward informing application to an extensive correspondence biological system mirrors its responsiveness to client requests and the unique idea of the computerized scene.

Looking forward, WhatsApp's direction seems ready for proceeded with development and advancement. The incorporation of arising advances, for example, computerized reasoning and expanded reality, holds the commitment of improving client encounters and opening new roads for correspondence. The stage's capacity to remain at the cutting edge of mechanical progressions will probably decide its proceeded with predominance in the worldwide correspondence scene.

In this investigation of WhatsApp's worldwide excursion, we will explore through the key achievements, difficulties, and developments that have formed its story. From its unassuming starting points to its ongoing status as a universal specialized device, WhatsApp's story is interwoven with the more extensive story of mechanical development and cultural change. As we unwind the layers of WhatsApp's worldwide mastery, we gain bits of knowledge into the unpredictable dance among innovation and human association in the 21st 100 years.

1.1 Overview of WhatsApp's rise to global prominence

The climb of WhatsApp to worldwide unmistakable quality addresses a captivating excursion through the development of computerized correspondence in the 21st hundred years. Brought into the world in 2009 as a brainchild of Jan Koum and Brian Acton, WhatsApp started its direction as a basic informing application. Its beginning was established in the pioneers' vision to make an effective and easy to understand stage for correspondence, especially focusing on the developing rush of cell phone clients.

At its origin, WhatsApp took care of the essential requirement for texting. With a moderate plan and clear usefulness, the application built up forward momentum by offering a dependable option in contrast to customary SMS. Its allure lay in its cross-stage similarity, empowering clients to impart consistently across different gadgets and working frameworks. This effortlessness and cross-gadget usefulness turned into the foundation of WhatsApp's prosperity.

The stage's initial development can be ascribed to its essential way to deal with tending to client problem areas. As cell phones multiplied worldwide, making a requirement for savvy and moment correspondence, WhatsApp arose as a convenient arrangement. Its reception was quick, with clients perceiving the application's capability to rise above the impediments of customary informing administrations.

WhatsApp's ascent picked up additional speed as it took advantage of the outlook of the cell phone time. The application's similarity with Wi-Fi and portable information networks gave clients a practical and effective method for correspondence. The planning of WhatsApp's send off lined up with the remarkable development of cell phone proprietorship, particularly in developing business sectors, where the application immediately turned into a staple for computerized correspondence.

In 2014, a turning point happened that would shape WhatsApp's direction in a significant manner. Facebook, drove by Imprint Zuckerberg, procured WhatsApp for a faltering $19 billion, stamping one of the biggest tech acquisitions ever. This obtaining mixed significant monetary assets into WhatsApp as well as adjusted it to the more extensive Facebook biological system. The mix with Facebook achieved cooperative energies that improved WhatsApp's capacities and situated it as an essential player in the developing scene of virtual entertainment and correspondence.

The marriage of WhatsApp with Facebook presented a heap of potential outcomes. Cross-stage joining with other Facebook-claimed administrations, like Instagram, made a consistent computerized biological system. Clients could now share content easily across stages, growing the range and effect of WhatsApp. This reconciliation likewise denoted the start of WhatsApp's change from an independent informing application to a multi-layered correspondence center.

Security arose as a focal topic in WhatsApp's story, recognizing it from other informing stages. The execution of start to finish encryption turned into a sign of WhatsApp's obligation to client protection. This encryption guaranteed that main the expected beneficiaries could get to the substance of messages, safeguarding clients from outer investigation. In a time where information protection concerns were on the ascent, WhatsApp's accentuation on secure and confidential correspondence resounded with a worldwide crowd.

The worldwide reception of WhatsApp was not simply a consequence of mechanical development but rather likewise an impression of its flexibility to different social and semantic settings. The stage's multilingual help and instinctive connection point rose above language hindrances, making it available to clients around the world. This inclusivity added to WhatsApp's general allure, cultivating a feeling of association among individuals from various semantic and social foundations.

WhatsApp's excursion to worldwide control was described by a progression of vital developments and element presentations. The stage's consistent advancement kept it on the ball, guaranteeing that it met the developing requirements of clients. Highlights, for example, voice messages, video calls, and the capacity to share interactive media content enhanced the client experience, changing WhatsApp into a flexible specialized device.

Organizations, perceiving the stage's universality, started to use WhatsApp as an immediate and productive channel for client commitment. The presentation of WhatsApp Business in 2018 formalized this pattern, furnishing endeavors with devices to make business profiles, computerize reactions, and manage exchanges inside the stage. WhatsApp's development into a business specialized instrument highlighted its versatility to the changing elements of computerized trade.

The flood in overall clients was not without challenges. WhatsApp confronted examination over protection concerns, especially with respect to the treatment of client information. The stage answered proactively, carrying out measures to improve client command over security settings and teach clients on accepted procedures. The obligation to straightforwardness and client strengthening became essential to WhatsApp's system in exploring the perplexing scene of information security.

Falsehood and the spread of phony news represented one more test for WhatsApp as its client base extended. The stage took purposeful endeavors to control the scattering of misleading data, presenting highlights like message sending limits and collaborating with truth really taking a look at associations. These drives expected to find some kind of harmony between cultivating open correspondence and forestalling the abuse of the stage for pernicious purposes.

WhatsApp's effect stretched out past metropolitan habitats and created countries, arriving at far off regions and underserved networks. In arising economies where conventional correspondence foundation was missing, WhatsApp turned into a help, interfacing individuals to the more extensive world. This democratization of correspondence assumed a significant part in connecting computerized partitions and cultivating inclusivity on a worldwide scale.

The stage's strength and versatility were additionally scrutinized during worldwide occasions that reshaped the manner in which individuals lived and worked. The Coronavirus pandemic, specifically, highlighted the significance of computerized correspondence, with WhatsApp filling in as an imperative device for remote work, virtual social cooperations, and dispersing urgent data. The pandemic sped up the mix of advanced correspondence into different parts of day to day existence, setting WhatsApp's job as a basic stage in the new ordinary.

WhatsApp's introduction to monetary administrations with the presentation of WhatsApp Pay added another aspect to its abilities. The component permitted clients to make monetary exchanges inside the application, situating WhatsApp as a specialized device as well as a stage for monetary communications.

This move lined up with the more extensive pattern of computerized installment reception and situated WhatsApp as a player in the developing scene of fintech.

As we ponder WhatsApp's ascent to worldwide noticeable quality, it becomes obvious that its prosperity is complicatedly attached to its capacity to advance with the changing tides of innovation and cultural necessities. From a humble informing application to an exhaustive correspondence biological system, WhatsApp's process mirrors the more extensive story of computerized change in the 21st 100 years. Its effect on how people, organizations, and networks interface and convey fills in as a demonstration of the extraordinary force of innovation in forming the manner in which we communicate in an undeniably interconnected world.

Looking forward, WhatsApp's direction seems ready for proceeded with advancement and development. The combination of arising advances, for example, computerized reasoning and increased reality, holds the possibility to reclassify the limits of correspondence. WhatsApp's capacity to remain at the front line of mechanical progressions will decide its importance in a steadily changing advanced scene.

In this outline of WhatsApp's ascent to worldwide conspicuousness, we have navigated the key achievements, difficulties, and developments that have characterized its excursion. From its unassuming starting points to its ongoing status as a worldwide correspondence goliath, WhatsApp's story epitomizes the development of computerized correspondence and its significant effect on the manner in which we associate, convey, and lead business in the cutting edge period.

1.2 Historical context of messaging platforms

To understand the verifiable setting of informing stages and value the meaning of WhatsApp's ascent to worldwide unmistakable quality, it is basic to dig into the advancement of correspondence innovations throughout recent many years. The excursion from traditional method for correspondence to the period of texting reflects mechanical headways as well as the changing elements of human cooperation in the advanced age.

The foundations of informing stages can be followed back to the beginning of PC intervened correspondence. During the 1980s and 1990s, as PCs turned out to be more common, email arose as a progressive instrument for nonconcurrent correspondence. While email was a huge jump forward, it missing the mark on promptness and immediacy that portray present day informing stages. The ongoing, simultaneous nature of correspondence was at this point to be completely understood.

The appearance of Short Message Administration (SMS) in the mid 1990s denoted a significant crossroads in the development of portable correspondence. SMS, ordinarily known as message informing, permitted clients to send short message based messages between cell phones.

While SMS turned out to be massively well known and boundless, it was obliged by character limits, and each message caused an expense, making a hindrance for broad use.

The scene of informing went through a seismic shift with the ascent of web based informing stages in the last part of the 1990s and mid 2000s. Administrations like AOL Moment Courier (Point), ICQ, and MSN Courier prepared for online continuous correspondence. These stages, dominatingly utilized on PCs, presented the idea of texting, empowering clients to take part in message based discussions with companions and associates continuously.

The progress from work area driven to versatile driven correspondence was advanced with the appearance of cell phones in the last part of the 2000s. The incorporation of cell phones with web network established the groundwork for another time of informing stages. BlackBerry Courier (BBM) acquired unmistakable quality as one of the early versatile driven informing administrations, benefiting from the ubiquity of BlackBerry cell phones.

The year 2009 ended up being a turning point with the send off of WhatsApp. Established by Jan Koum and Brian Acton, WhatsApp set off on a mission to address the weaknesses of existing informing stages. At its center, WhatsApp planned to give an easy to understand, financially savvy, and quick method for correspondence. The application's prosperity was energized by its cross-stage similarity, which permitted clients to consistently send messages across various working frameworks and gadgets.

WhatsApp's rise corresponded with the fast multiplication of cell phones worldwide. As additional individuals embraced cell phones, the interest for moment and financially savvy correspondence arrangements took off. WhatsApp made up for a pivotal shortcoming by offering a dependable option in contrast to conventional SMS, furnishing clients with a stage that joined the comfort of text informing with the promptness of ongoing correspondence.

The obtaining of WhatsApp by Facebook in 2014 denoted an essential move in the scene of informing stages. Facebook's securing approved the significance of informing administrations as well as flagged a change in center from customary informal communication to additional close and quick types of correspondence. This obtaining laid the preparation for the coordination of WhatsApp into the more extensive Facebook biological system.

The verifiable setting of informing stages additionally incorporates the serious scene and the rise of other outstanding players. Wire, Signal, WeChat, and Viber are among the stages that have added to the broadening of the informing biological system. Every stage brought its one of a kind elements, taking care of explicit client inclinations and necessities. Wire, for example, stressed protection and security, while WeChat incorporated informing with a great many administrations, including long range interpersonal communication and monetary exchanges.

As informing stages kept on advancing, the significance of protection and security turned out to be progressively unmistakable. The disclosure of far and wide observation and information breaks highlighted the weakness of advanced correspondence. This uplifted consciousness of protection concerns impacted the plan and elements of informing stages, with an accentuation on start to finish encryption and client controlled security settings.

The worldwide scene of informing stages is additionally molded by local inclinations and administrative conditions. WeChat, for instance, overwhelms the Chinese market, offering a far reaching biological system that stretches out past informing to incorporate long range interpersonal communication, internet business, and monetary administrations. LINE, a famous informing application in Japan and other Asian nations, likewise coordinates informing with a different exhibit of administrations.

The verifiable setting of informing stages mirrors the unique transaction between mechanical advancement, client conduct, and cultural patterns. The development from email and SMS to the period of texting on cell phones represents the tenacious quest for more quick, productive, and expressive methods of correspondence. Informing stages, basically, have turned into the courses through which people, organizations, and networks produce associations in an undeniably interconnected world.

Looking at the verifiable direction of informing stages likewise reveals insight into the job they play in molding social communications. The shift from one-way correspondence channels, like email, to the intuitive and ongoing nature of informing stages means a more extensive cultural progress toward additional participatory and connecting with types of correspondence. The capacity to share sight and sound substance, participate in bunch discussions, and articulate one's thoughts through emoticons and stickers has become essential to the advanced correspondence experience.

The ascent of informing stages is profoundly interlaced with the more extensive story of the advanced age. The universality of cell phones, the multiplication of fast web, and the intermingling of different computerized administrations have made an environment where informing stages act as focal center points for correspondence, data sharing, and even conditional exercises. The verifiable setting gives a focal point through which we can see the value in the groundbreaking effect of informing stages on the manner in which we interface, work together, and impart in the 21st hundred years.

WhatsApp's excursion to worldwide noticeable quality inside this verifiable setting is a demonstration of its capacity to address developing correspondence needs and influence mechanical progressions. The stage's prosperity isn't just a consequence of its mechanical highlights yet in addition comprehension of the social and social elements shape correspondence inclinations.

As we explore the complicated landscape of informing stages, we perceive that WhatsApp's climb addresses a section in the bigger story of how computerized correspondence has developed, associating individuals across borders and reclassifying the manner in which we experience the world.

1.3 Brief examination of early challenges and successes

In the beginning phases of its presence, WhatsApp experienced a large number of difficulties as it tried to set up a good foundation for itself as a superior informing stage. The actual idea of the application's beginning, established in the vision of Jan Koum and Brian Acton, was a reaction to the limits and burdens of conventional informing frameworks. The underlying test lay in persuading clients to move from dug in specialized techniques to a moderately obscure and untested stage.

At the core of WhatsApp's incentive was giving a financially savvy option in contrast to SMS. In our current reality where messaging brought about charges per message and character limits compelled correspondence, WhatsApp's commitment of limitless free informing reverberated with clients. Nonetheless, getting out from under instilled propensities and persuading a worldwide client base to take on another informing worldview required mechanical development as well as successful correspondence of the application's advantages.

Additionally, the serious scene was not without hindrances. Laid out players in the informing field, including SMS and other web based informing administrations, represented a huge test. Persuading clients to embrace another stage implied defeating the inactivity related with existing propensities and the organization impacts that leaned toward broadly embraced administrations. WhatsApp's prosperity relied on its capacity to situate itself as a prevalent and more proficient option quickly.

The worldwide extension of WhatsApp confronted extra obstacles, with varieties in portable framework and information costs across various districts. In developing business sectors, where cell phone entrance was on the ascent however information plans were in many cases cost-restrictive, the test was to show the worth of the application convincingly. WhatsApp's lightweight plan and effective utilization of information, joined with its cross-stage similarity, assumed a vital part in conquering these deterrents and making it open to clients around the world.

One of the basic achievement factors during these early stages was the accentuation on effortlessness and unwavering quality. WhatsApp focused on a perfect and instinctive UI, guaranteeing that even people new to trend setting innovation could undoubtedly explore the application. The obligation to dependability was similarly principal; clients expected to believe that their messages would be conveyed instantly and reliably, paying little mind to geological area or organization conditions.

WhatsApp's initial victories can be ascribed to its adroit route of these difficulties. The choice to shun commercials and take on a membership model, where clients paid an ostensible expense after the primary year of free help, kept an easy to understand insight without the interruption of promotions. This income model was imaginative as well as lined up with the application's obligation to focusing on client experience over forceful adaptation procedures.

In addition, WhatsApp's commitment to security put it aside from its counterparts. At the point when worries about computerized security were raising, WhatsApp executed start to finish encryption, guaranteeing that main the expected beneficiaries could get to the substance of messages. This obligation to client security reverberated with a worldwide crowd progressively careful about information breaks and unapproved admittance to individual data.

The choice to zero in on informing as the center usefulness of the application, without capitulating to highlight swell, was another essential achievement. While contenders jumbled their foundation with a horde of highlights, WhatsApp stayed resolute in its devotion to giving a solid and clear informing experience. This center smoothed out the client experience as well as added to the application's productivity and inescapable reception.

As WhatsApp built up some decent forward movement, its effect was especially articulated in areas where customary correspondence framework was less powerful. In arising economies, the application turned into a groundbreaking power, empowering people to impart across borders without causing extravagant expenses. The lightweight plan of WhatsApp, upgraded for changing organization conditions, made it a practical answer for clients in regions with restricted network.

The significant defining moment in WhatsApp's direction accompanied its procurement by Facebook in 2014. The $19 billion arrangement not just shot WhatsApp into the higher classes of tech acquisitions yet additionally gave the application the assets and vital sponsorship of perhaps of the biggest social medium stages. The securing denoted an acknowledgment of the extraordinary force of informing administrations in the developing scene of computerized correspondence.

The mix with Facebook achieved the two open doors and difficulties. On the positive side, WhatsApp accessed the immense assets and ability of Facebook, considering sped up advancement and development. The cross-stage coordination with other Facebook-possessed administrations, like Instagram, extended the scope of WhatsApp and situated it as a vital piece of a bigger computerized environment.

In any case, the procurement additionally raised worries about the possible effect on client security and the independence of WhatsApp. The application's obligation to start to finish encryption confronted investigation, and clients were watchful about keeping up with the protection includes that had been key to WhatsApp's allure. Adjusting the advantages of mix with Facebook and safeguarding the application's character turned into a sensitive test for WhatsApp following the obtaining.

In exploring these difficulties, WhatsApp kept on advancing. The presentation of voice informing, video calls, and media sharing capacities expanded the application's usefulness while holding its easy to use plan. These elements stayed up with developing client assumptions as well as situated WhatsApp as a far reaching specialized instrument equipped for working with a great many collaborations past text-based informing.

WhatsApp's prosperity was additionally pushed by its capacity to adjust to different etymological and social settings. The application's multilingual help and instinctive plan made it available to clients from various language foundations. This inclusivity added to its worldwide allure, cultivating a feeling of association among people and networks across phonetic partitions.

The stage's progress in developing business sectors, where it turned into an essential method of correspondence for people and organizations, displayed its flexibility. WhatsApp Business, presented in 2018, formalized the application's job in business correspondence. It gave apparatuses to ventures to make business profiles, computerize reactions, and draw in with clients straightforwardly through the stage. WhatsApp's development into a business specialized instrument highlighted its versatility to the changing elements of computerized trade.

As WhatsApp tended to these difficulties and set its situation as a worldwide correspondence monster, it all the while faced new obstacles. The developing worries about deception and the spread of phony news on the stage turned into a conspicuous issue. The start to finish encryption, while safeguarding client security, additionally presented difficulties in checking and controling the dispersal of misleading data.

WhatsApp answered these difficulties with a progression of measures pointed toward finding some kind of harmony among protection and fighting falsehood. The presentation of message sending limits, alongside instructive missions to advance computerized proficiency, mirrored WhatsApp's obligation to moderating the adverse consequence of its foundation. These endeavors featured the advancing job of informing stages in the time of data scattering and the moral contemplations that accompany it.

The year 2020 brought phenomenal difficulties with the worldwide Coronavirus pandemic, essentially modifying the elements of correspondence and complementing the significance of computerized stages. WhatsApp, as a dependable and quick method for correspondence, assumed a vital part in interfacing people, families, and organizations during a time of lockdowns and social removing. The pandemic highlighted the basic job of advanced specialized devices in working with remote work, virtual social associations, and the dispersal of critical data.

In the midst of the continuous difficulties, WhatsApp's introduction to monetary administrations with WhatsApp Pay added another aspect to its capacities. The element empowered clients to make monetary exchanges straightforwardly inside the application, lining up with the more extensive pattern of computerized installment reception. WhatsApp's entrance into the fintech space denoted an essential extension of its administrations, situating the stage as a specialized device as well as a facilitator of monetary cooperations.

As we ponder the early difficulties and triumphs of WhatsApp, it is clear that the application's process is set apart by a constant course of variation and development. From beating protection from change and securing itself as a suitable option in contrast to SMS to exploring the intricacies of worldwide extension and security concerns, WhatsApp's development mirrors a nuanced comprehension of client needs and the powerful scene of computerized correspondence.

WhatsApp's obligation to effortlessness, dependability, and client protection has been a reliable subject over now is the right time. The application's prosperity lies in its mechanical elements as well as in its capacity to reverberate with a different worldwide crowd. The tale of WhatsApp's ascent to worldwide unmistakable quality fills in as a demonstration of the groundbreaking force of innovation in forming the manner in which we impart, interface, and direct business in the cutting edge period. As the application keeps on advancing, its process mirrors the more extensive story of computerized change and the basic job of informing stages in the texture of contemporary society.

Chapter 2

The Birth of WhatsApp

In the immense scene of mechanical advancement, certain developments arise as turning points, modifying the texture of human correspondence. The introduction of WhatsApp remains as a demonstration of the groundbreaking force of innovation, reshaping the manner in which individuals interface and convey in the computerized age.

It was in 2009 that WhatsApp, an informing stage, made its unassuming presentation. Established by Jan Koum and Brian Acton, two previous workers of Hurray!, WhatsApp expected to address a straightforward yet critical need — working with correspondence in a quick, solid, and practical way. Much to their dismay that their creation would reform the manner in which billions of individuals across the globe communicate.

The beginning of WhatsApp can be followed back to Jan Koum's life as a youngster in Ukraine. Brought into the world in a little town, Koum encountered the difficulties of correspondence in a country that was frequently disconnected from the remainder of the world. This early openness to the significance of remaining associated regardless of actual distances sowed the seed for what might later become WhatsApp.

In the beginning of the web, Koum moved to the US with his loved ones. Notwithstanding, the battles endured, and they depended on food stamps to earn barely enough to get by. These difficulties imparted in Koum an assurance to make an answer that would rise above monetary boundaries and work with correspondence for everybody.

The excursion of WhatsApp started with Koum and Acton's joint effort at Yippee! where they saw the elements of the tech business firsthand. It was during this time that they distinguished a hole on the lookout — a requirement for a correspondence stage that rose above the impediments of existing choices.

In 2009, Koum and Acton revealed WhatsApp to the world. The application offered a straightforward, easy to use interface, permitting individuals to send instant messages, photographs, and recordings without causing the over the top expenses related with conventional SMS administrations. This progressive way to deal with informing immediately built up some decent forward momentum, and clients ran to WhatsApp as an option in contrast to costly and frequently questionable specialized strategies.

The outcome of WhatsApp can be credited to its obligation to client protection and information security. Not at all like other informing stages, WhatsApp executed start to finish encryption, guaranteeing that main the expected beneficiaries could get to the messages.

This obligation to protection resounded with clients, particularly when worries about advanced security were on the ascent.

As the client base developed, WhatsApp kept on improving, presenting elements, for example, voice informing, bunch talks, and video calls. These increments further set WhatsApp's situation as an extensive correspondence stage, obliging an extensive variety of client inclinations.

The defining moment for WhatsApp came in 2014 when Facebook, drove by Imprint Zuckerberg, procured the informing monster for a faltering $19 billion. The securing caused a stir in the tech business, igniting banters about the valuation of informing applications. Nonetheless, Zuckerberg saw the potential for WhatsApp to supplement Facebook's current administrations and extend its span universally.

Under Facebook's proprietorship, WhatsApp went through essential extensions and updates. The client base took off, arriving at billions of dynamic clients around the world. The reconciliation of WhatsApp with other Facebook-possessed stages, for example, Instagram, opened new roads for cross-stage correspondence, further improving the client experience.

Notwithstanding its fleeting ascent, WhatsApp confronted its portion of difficulties. Security concerns, changes to the stage's help out, and banters over information offering to Facebook blended debates. Clients communicated fears about the expected split the difference of their security, prompting shifts in inclinations and the investigation of elective informing stages.

The advancement of WhatsApp likewise met with more extensive cultural changes. The stage assumed a significant part in political developments, social activism, and emergency correspondence. Its capacity to work with moment, far and wide correspondence became obvious during occasions, for example, the Middle Easterner Spring and different fights all over the planet. WhatsApp turned into a device for putting together, preparing, and dispersing data continuously.

The business scene additionally felt the effect of WhatsApp's universality. The stage developed past private correspondence, turning into a necessary piece of business systems. WhatsApp Business, a devoted stage for ventures, permitted organizations to interface with clients, give client care, and manage exchanges consistently.

As innovation progressed, so did the highlights of WhatsApp. The presentation of WhatsApp Pay permitted clients to send and get cash straightforwardly through the application, changing it into a multi-layered stage that took special care of different requirements. The incorporation of Man-made consciousness (computer based intelligence) and chatbots further improved the client experience, making collaborations more instinctive and customized.

The impact of WhatsApp reached out to different areas, including instruction, medical services, and money. The stage's openness and flexibility made it an important instrument for remote learning, telemedicine, and monetary exchanges. This far reaching joining into day to day existence highlighted the groundbreaking effect of WhatsApp on assorted parts of society.

Nonetheless, the excursion of WhatsApp was not without obstacles. Administrative difficulties, worries about deception spreading through the stage, and contest from arising rivals introduced continuous difficulties. The need to figure out some kind of harmony between development, client protection, and consistence with administrative systems turned into a fragile dance for WhatsApp and its parent organization, Facebook.

Amidst these difficulties, the year 2021 denoted a huge second for WhatsApp as it commended its twelfth commemoration. The stage had made considerable progress from its modest starting points, developing into a worldwide correspondence behemoth. The client base had extended dramatically, including people, organizations, and networks across the world.

Looking forward, the fate of WhatsApp remained interlaced with the more extensive scene of innovation. The proceeded with development of correspondence advancements, the approach of 5G, and the investigation of new outskirts, for example, expanded reality vowed to shape the direction of WhatsApp in the years to come. The stage's capacity to adjust to evolving patterns, address client concerns, and enhance in light of arising advances would decide its proceeded with importance in the unique computerized environment.

The tradition of WhatsApp reached out past its job as an informing stage; it encapsulated the soul of development, strength, and the democratization of correspondence. From its beginnings in a little town in Ukraine to its status as a worldwide correspondence goliath, WhatsApp's process reflected the extraordinary force of innovation in molding the manner in which individuals interface and communicate.

All in all, the introduction of WhatsApp denoted a vital crossroads throughout the entire existence of correspondence innovation. From its commencement as an answer for the provokes of remaining associated across distances to its development into a worldwide correspondence force to be reckoned with, WhatsApp reshaped the way people, organizations, and networks cooperated in the computerized age. The stage's obligation to protection, constant advancement, and flexibility to cultural changes impelled it to the front of the informing scene. As WhatsApp explored difficulties, celebrated achievements, and embraced new innovations, its process turned into a demonstration of the persevering through effect of development on the texture of human association. The tale of WhatsApp isn't only one of an informing application; it is a story of how innovation can rise above limits, bring individuals closer, and reclassify the conceivable outcomes of correspondence in a consistently developing world.

2.1 Background on the founders and their vision

In the immense scene of mechanical advancement, certain developments arise as turning points, modifying the texture of human correspondence. The introduction of WhatsApp remains as a demonstration of the groundbreaking force of innovation, reshaping the manner in which individuals interface and convey in the computerized age.

It was in 2009 that WhatsApp, an informing stage, made its unassuming presentation. Established by Jan Koum and Brian Acton, two previous workers of Hurray!, WhatsApp expected to address a straightforward yet critical need — working with correspondence in a quick, solid, and practical way. Much to their dismay that their creation would reform the manner in which billions of individuals across the globe communicate.

The beginning of WhatsApp can be followed back to Jan Koum's life as a youngster in Ukraine. Brought into the world in a little town, Koum encountered the difficulties of correspondence in a country that was frequently disconnected from the remainder of the world. This early openness to the significance of remaining associated regardless of actual distances sowed the seed for what might later become WhatsApp.

In the beginning of the web, Koum moved to the US with his loved ones. Notwithstanding, the battles endured, and they depended on food stamps to earn barely enough to get by. These difficulties imparted in Koum an assurance to make an answer that would rise above monetary boundaries and work with correspondence for everybody.

The excursion of WhatsApp started with Koum and Acton's joint effort at Yippee! where they saw the elements of the tech business firsthand. It was during this time that they distinguished a hole on the lookout — a requirement for a correspondence stage that rose above the impediments of existing choices.

In 2009, Koum and Acton revealed WhatsApp to the world. The application offered a straightforward, easy to use interface, permitting individuals to send instant messages, photographs, and recordings without causing the over the top expenses related with conventional SMS administrations. This progressive way to deal with informing immediately built up some decent forward momentum, and clients ran to WhatsApp as an option in contrast to costly and frequently questionable specialized strategies.

The outcome of WhatsApp can be credited to its obligation to client protection and information security. Not at all like other informing stages, WhatsApp executed start to finish encryption, guaranteeing that main the expected beneficiaries could get to the messages. This obligation to protection resounded with clients, particularly when worries about advanced security were on the ascent.

As the client base developed, WhatsApp kept on improving, presenting elements, for example, voice informing, bunch talks, and video calls. These increments further set WhatsApp's situation as an extensive correspondence stage, obliging an extensive variety of client inclinations.

The defining moment for WhatsApp came in 2014 when Facebook, drove by Imprint Zuckerberg, procured the informing monster for a faltering $19 billion. The securing caused a stir in the tech business, igniting banters about the valuation of informing applications. Nonetheless, Zuckerberg saw the potential for WhatsApp to supplement Facebook's current administrations and extend its span universally.

Under Facebook's proprietorship, WhatsApp went through essential extensions and updates. The client base took off, arriving at billions of dynamic clients around the world. The reconciliation of WhatsApp with other Facebook-possessed stages, for example, Instagram, opened new roads for cross-stage correspondence, further improving the client experience.

Notwithstanding its fleeting ascent, WhatsApp confronted its portion of difficulties. Security concerns, changes to the stage's help out, and banters over information offering to Facebook blended debates. Clients communicated fears about the expected split the difference of their security, prompting shifts in inclinations and the investigation of elective informing stages.

The advancement of WhatsApp likewise met with more extensive cultural changes. The stage assumed a significant part in political developments, social activism, and emergency correspondence. Its capacity to work with moment, far and wide correspondence became obvious during occasions, for example, the Middle Easterner Spring and different fights all over the planet. WhatsApp turned into a device for putting together, preparing, and dispersing data continuously.

The business scene additionally felt the effect of WhatsApp's universality. The stage developed past private correspondence, turning into a necessary piece of business systems. WhatsApp Business, a devoted stage for ventures, permitted organizations to interface with clients, give client care, and manage exchanges consistently.

As innovation progressed, so did the highlights of WhatsApp. The presentation of WhatsApp Pay permitted clients to send and get cash straightforwardly through the application, changing it into a multi-layered stage that took special care of different requirements. The incorporation of Man-made consciousness (computer based intelligence) and chatbots further improved the client experience, making collaborations more instinctive and customized.

The impact of WhatsApp reached out to different areas, including instruction, medical services, and money. The stage's openness and flexibility made it an important instrument for remote learning, telemedicine, and monetary exchanges. This far reaching joining into day to day existence highlighted the groundbreaking effect of WhatsApp on assorted parts of society.

Nonetheless, the excursion of WhatsApp was not without obstacles. Administrative difficulties, worries about deception spreading through the stage, and contest from arising rivals introduced continuous difficulties. The need to figure out some kind of harmony between development, client protection, and consistence with administrative systems turned into a fragile dance for WhatsApp and its parent organization, Facebook.

Amidst these difficulties, the year 2021 denoted a huge second for WhatsApp as it commended its twelfth commemoration. The stage had made considerable progress from its modest starting points, developing into a worldwide correspondence behemoth. The client base had extended dramatically, including people, organizations, and networks across the world.

Looking forward, the fate of WhatsApp remained interlaced with the more extensive scene of innovation. The proceeded with development of correspondence advancements, the approach of 5G, and the investigation of new outskirts, for example, expanded reality vowed to shape the direction of WhatsApp in the years to come. The stage's capacity to adjust to evolving patterns, address client concerns, and enhance in light of arising advances would decide its proceeded with importance in the unique computerized environment.

The tradition of WhatsApp reached out past its job as an informing stage; it encapsulated the soul of development, strength, and the democratization of correspondence. From its beginnings in a little town in Ukraine to its status as a worldwide correspondence goliath, WhatsApp's process reflected the extraordinary force of innovation in molding the manner in which individuals interface and communicate.

All in all, the introduction of WhatsApp denoted a vital crossroads throughout the entire existence of correspondence innovation. From its commencement as an answer for the provokes of remaining associated across distances to its development into a worldwide correspondence force to be reckoned with, WhatsApp reshaped the way people, organizations, and networks cooperated in the computerized age. The stage's obligation to protection, constant advancement, and flexibility to cultural changes impelled it to the front of the informing scene. As WhatsApp explored difficulties, celebrated achievements, and embraced new innovations, its process turned into a demonstration of the persevering through effect of development on the texture of human association. The tale of WhatsApp isn't only one of an informing application; it is a story of how innovation can rise above limits, bring individuals closer, and reclassify the conceivable outcomes of correspondence in a consistently developing world.

2.2 The development and launch of the messaging platform

The turn of events and send off of WhatsApp denoted a huge achievement in the development of computerized correspondence. From its unassuming starting points as a thought brought about by Jan Koum and Brian Acton to its possible development as a worldwide correspondence monster, the excursion of WhatsApp was described by advancement, diligence, and a guarantee to tending to the advancing necessities of clients in the computerized age.

The underlying phases of WhatsApp's improvement can be followed back to the encounters and experiences acquired by Jan Koum during his time at Hurray!. Koum's openness to the elements of the tech business, combined with his firsthand comprehension of the difficulties of correspondence in a worldwide setting, established the groundwork for what might later become WhatsApp.

In 2009, Koum and Acton formally sent off WhatsApp as an informing stage intended to give a straightforward, solid, and practical answer for the correspondence hindrances of the time. The beginning of WhatsApp was a reaction to the restrictions of existing specialized strategies, especially the significant expenses related with Short Message Administration (SMS) and the instability of other informing stages.

The center vision behind WhatsApp was to democratize correspondence, making it open to people across financial layers. Koum, drawing from his own encounters of monetary difficulty and restricted admittance to correspondence, imagined a stage that would rise above the monetary boundaries related with customary informing administrations. The objective was to make a device that would enable individuals to interface with each other consistently, regardless of their financial foundation.

The improvement of WhatsApp started with an emphasis on effortlessness and productivity. Koum and Acton intended to make an easy to use interface that would permit people to send instant messages, photographs, and recordings without the requirement for costly information plans or cell network charges. This obligation to straightforwardness was obvious in the stage's plan, which focused on usability and a perfect, natural connection point.

In the good 'ol days, WhatsApp worked with a lean group, with Koum and Acton taking on different jobs to keep the stage functional. Their involved methodology and devotion to the vision of WhatsApp set the vibe for the organization culture — an ethos that underlined client experience, security, and a pledge to offering a significant support.

The send off of WhatsApp was a calm yet effective passage into the universe of informing stages. Not at all like numerous tech new businesses that earn consideration through ostentatious send-offs, WhatsApp depended on the intrinsic worth it gave to clients. The stage's capacity to permit people to impart without the monetary weight of customary informing administrations immediately resounded with clients, prompting natural development and verbal exchange references.

One of the key variables adding to WhatsApp's prosperity was its obligation to client protection and information security. Indeed, even in its beginning phases, WhatsApp executed start to finish encryption, guaranteeing that main the expected beneficiaries could get to the messages. This obligation to protection turned into a sign of WhatsApp's personality and assumed a urgent part in acquiring the trust of clients.

As the client base extended, WhatsApp proceeded to emphasize and work on its elements. The stage presented voice informing, permitting clients to send sound messages notwithstanding message and media. Bunch talk usefulness was additionally added, empowering clients to all the while speak with different individuals. These increases mirrored WhatsApp's responsiveness to client needs and its obligation to giving an exhaustive correspondence experience.

In 2014, a turning point happened in WhatsApp's excursion when Facebook gained the informing stage for $19 billion. The securing caused a commotion in the tech business, with conversations about the valuation of an informing application arriving at uncommon levels. Nonetheless, Imprint Zuckerberg, the Chief of Facebook, perceived the essential worth of WhatsApp in upgrading Facebook's correspondence capacities and extending its client base universally.

Under Facebook's proprietorship, WhatsApp went through essential developments and updates. The incorporation with other Facebook-claimed stages, like Instagram, intended to make an additional durable and interconnected virtual entertainment biological system. While the securing brought assets and open doors for development, it additionally presented new difficulties, including worries about client protection, information sharing, and the stage's freedom inside the bigger Facebook environment.

The client base of WhatsApp kept on developing dramatically under Facebook's proprietorship, arriving at billions of dynamic clients around the world. The coordination of elements, for example, video calls and notices added new aspects to the stage, making it an informing application as well as a far reaching specialized instrument.

In any case, the procurement additionally provoked conversations about the possible effect on WhatsApp's ethos of client protection. WhatsApp had constructed its standing on being a safe and confidential informing stage, and any apparent split the difference in this space prompted examination and discussions. Clients communicated worries about the ramifications of information imparting to Facebook and the likely disintegration of the stage's obligation to start to finish encryption.

In the midst of these difficulties, Koum and Acton kept on driving WhatsApp, keeping up with their obligation to client security and experience. The stage developed to meet the changing necessities of clients, presenting elements, for example, WhatsApp Business to take care of the correspondence prerequisites of undertakings. This essential venture into the business domain mirrored WhatsApp's flexibility and versatility to different client requests.

The job of WhatsApp in cultural occasions turned out to be progressively obvious as the stage assumed an essential part in political developments, social activism, and emergency correspondence. The Middle Easterner Spring and different worldwide fights exhibited WhatsApp as a device for putting together, preparing, and dispersing data continuously.

The encoded idea of WhatsApp's informing framework gave a solid space to activists and coordinators to facilitate endeavors unafraid of reconnaissance.

Past individual correspondence, WhatsApp's effect stretched out to organizations and different areas. The stage's incorporation into day to day existence made it an important instrument for remote learning, telemedicine, and monetary exchanges. The presentation of WhatsApp Pay permitted clients to send and get cash straightforwardly through the application, changing it into a complex stage that took special care of different requirements.

Regardless of its triumphs, WhatsApp confronted its portion of difficulties. Changes to the stage's terms of administration started discussions, and worries about the spread of deception through the stage brought up issues about its part in molding public talk. The need to work out some kind of harmony between development, client security, and consistence with administrative systems turned into a fragile test for WhatsApp and its parent organization, Facebook.

The year 2021 denoted the twelfth commemoration of WhatsApp, a demonstration of its persevering through presence in the quickly developing scene of computerized correspondence. The festival of this achievement gave a chance to consider the stage's excursion, from a little startup addressing a particular need to a worldwide correspondence monster impacting the manner in which individuals associate and cooperate.

Looking forward, the eventual fate of WhatsApp remained interweaved with the more extensive direction of innovation. The proceeded with advancement of correspondence advancements, the approach of 5G, and the investigation of new wildernesses, for example, expanded reality vowed to shape WhatsApp's way in the years to come. The stage's capacity to adjust to evolving patterns, address client concerns, and improve in light of arising advancements would decide its proceeded with significance in the powerful computerized biological system.

2.3 Initial reception and early user adoption

The underlying gathering and early client reception of WhatsApp denoted an exceptional part in the stage's excursion, featuring the reverberation of its vision with clients all over the planet. Sent off in 2009 by Jan Koum and Brian Acton, WhatsApp meant to give a straightforward, solid, and savvy answer for the correspondence difficulties of the time. As clients embraced the stage, it became clear that WhatsApp had hit home by tending to an essential need in the developing scene of computerized correspondence.

In the good 'ol days, WhatsApp entered a serious market overwhelmed by conventional informing administrations and arising talk applications. Be that as it may, what put WhatsApp aside was its obligation to effortlessness and proficiency.

The stage offered a perfect, easy to understand interface that permitted people to send instant messages, photographs, and recordings without causing the significant expenses related with Short Message Administration (SMS) or encountering the impediments of other informing applications.

The underlying gathering of WhatsApp was portrayed by a calm yet significant section into the computerized correspondence space. Rather than depending on broad advertising efforts, WhatsApp depended on the intrinsic worth it gave to clients. The stage's capacity to address the monetary obstructions related with customary informing administrations immediately resounded with clients, prompting natural development and positive verbal exchange references.

One of the key elements adding to WhatsApp's initial achievement was its obligation to client protection and information security. Indeed, even in its early stages, WhatsApp executed start to finish encryption, guaranteeing that messages must be gotten to by the planned beneficiaries. This obligation to protection turned into a distinctive element of WhatsApp, separating it from other informing stages and gathering the trust of clients worried about the security of their computerized correspondences.

As the word spread about an informing stage that offered a solid and savvy option in contrast to existing choices, WhatsApp experienced fast client reception. People, particularly those in districts where the expense of customary SMS administrations represented a huge boundary to correspondence, embraced WhatsApp as a way to associate with loved ones without the weight of high costs.

The allure of WhatsApp reached out past financial contemplations. Its natural plan and direct usefulness made it open to clients across age gatherings and mechanical capability levels. Whether utilized for individual correspondence or planning bunch exercises, WhatsApp turned into a flexible instrument that took special care of an expansive range of client needs.

The stage's prosperity was additionally floated by its cross-stage similarity. Whats-App was accessible on different working frameworks, including iOS, Android, and later, even on internet browsers. This adaptability guaranteed that clients could flawlessly speak with others no matter what the gadgets they utilized, adding to the stage's all inclusive allure.

As WhatsApp got forward momentum, it turned out to be progressively obvious that the stage was an informing application as well as a groundbreaking power in the manner individuals conveyed. It tended to a widespread requirement for solid and reasonable correspondence, rising above geological and monetary boundaries. This intrinsic incentive powered the natural development of WhatsApp's client base.

The presentation of highlights past customary message informing additionally advanced the client experience and added to early reception. The consolidation of voice informing permitted clients to send sound messages, adding a powerful aspect to correspondence. Bunch talk usefulness worked with consistent coordination among different people, settling on it a well known decision for social and expert connections.

The early progress of WhatsApp can likewise be credited to its obligation to offering a support liberated from meddlesome promoting. Dissimilar to different stages that depended on promotion income, WhatsApp kept an emphasis on conveying a clean and advertisement free client experience. This choice reverberated with clients who valued the shortfall of problematic commercials in their correspondence space.

By 2011, only two years after its send off, WhatsApp had previously arrived at a critical achievement with more than a billion messages being sent day to day on the stage. This amazing volume of messages highlighted the quick reception and reconciliation of WhatsApp into the regular routines of clients. The stage's development direction was a demonstration of the general allure of a help that improved and democratized correspondence.

WhatsApp's effect was not restricted to individual clients. Organizations and associations perceived the capability of the stage as a specialized device. The capacity to make gatherings, share updates, and direction exercises continuously made WhatsApp a significant resource for different expert and local area situated purposes. The stage's flexibility added to its far and wide reception across different areas.

In 2014, WhatsApp confronted a huge defining moment when it was obtained by Facebook for $19 billion. While the procurement brought up issues about the valuation of an informing application, it likewise flagged another stage in WhatsApp's excursion. The assets and reach given by Facebook opened up new open doors for development, extension, and reconciliation with different stages inside the Facebook environment.

Under Facebook's possession, WhatsApp kept on developing while at the same time keeping up with its obligation to client protection. The client base extended dramatically, arriving at billions of dynamic clients around the world. The incorporation with other Facebook-possessed stages, like Instagram, expected to make an additional interconnected virtual entertainment environment, permitting clients to impart flawlessly across different administrations.

The progress of WhatsApp during its initial years can be credited to a few key variables. First and foremost, the stage tended to a substantial and broad requirement for reasonable and dependable correspondence. By offering a help that evaded the significant expenses of customary SMS, WhatsApp turned into an appealing choice for clients all over the planet, particularly in districts where monetary imperatives presented critical difficulties.

Furthermore, the obligation to client protection and information security put WhatsApp aside in a scene where worries about computerized protection were developing. The execution of start to finish encryption from the very outset laid out an underpinning of trust with clients, it were secure and private to guarantee them that their correspondences.

Thirdly, WhatsApp's instinctive plan and easy to use interface added to its far and wide reception. The stage's straightforwardness made it open to an expansive crowd, including the individuals who probably won't be know all about more intricate informing applications. This inclusivity assumed an essential part in the stage's quick development.

Moreover, WhatsApp's cross-stage similarity and obligation to conveying a promotion free encounter lined up with client inclinations. The stage's accessibility on different working frameworks and gadgets guaranteed that clients could flawlessly speak with one another, no matter what the gadgets they utilized.

The stage's effect went past individual correspondence to assume a urgent part in cultural occasions. WhatsApp arose as a device for sorting out and preparing individuals during political developments and social activism. Its scrambled informing framework gave a safe space to activists and coordinators to organize endeavors, share data, and impart unafraid of reconnaissance.

As WhatsApp turned into a necessary piece of day to day existence, organizations perceived its true capacity as a specialized instrument. The presentation of WhatsApp Business further worked with the communication among organizations and clients, empowering ventures to give client service, share updates, and manage exchanges through the stage.

In spite of its initial achievement, WhatsApp confronted its portion of difficulties. The progress to Facebook proprietorship achieved changes and discussions about the likely effect on client protection. Worries about information imparting to Facebook and the coordination of WhatsApp into the bigger Facebook biological system incited conversations about the stage's autonomy and its capacity to keep up with its obligation to protection.

Changes to WhatsApp's help out in 2021 ignited discussions and worries among clients. The refreshed approach included arrangements for information imparting to Facebook, prompting worries about the expected split the difference of client protection. The backfire provoked WhatsApp to explain its protection practices and postpone the execution of the new approach, featuring the significance clients put on protection and information security.

The early client reception of WhatsApp not just mirrored its capacity to address a key need yet additionally its effect on molding the scene of computerized correspondence. The stage's development reflected the more extensive shift toward computerized correspondence stages as essential channels for remaining associated, both actually and expertly.

Chapter 3

Features and Evolution

In the terrific embroidery of human advancement, the unending walk of innovation has woven many-sided designs across the ages. From the simple apparatuses of our precursors to the confounding exhibit of headways in the 21st hundred years, the direction of advancement has been both steady and groundbreaking. As we explore the immense scene representing things to come, it becomes basic to take apart the elements and development of innovation, understanding how it shapes and is formed by the human experience.

One of the characterizing highlights of the mechanical scene in the 22nd century is the consistent coordination of man-made consciousness (artificial intelligence) into each feature of day to day existence. Simulated intelligence, when a domain of hypothesis and modern dreams, has turned into the bedrock of human life. The development of artificial intelligence has been set apart by dramatic development, pushed by the assembly of enormous information, high level calculations, and exceptional figuring power. In 2150, simulated intelligence isn't only a device; it is a universal presence, an undetectable hand that aides and upgrades the working of social orders.

The combination of artificial intelligence with other arising advancements has brought about the period of hyperconnectivity. The Web of Things (IoT) has risen above its initial conceptualization, developing into a tremendous organization where each gadget, from the minutest sensor to the most complex hardware, is interconnected. This interchange of simulated intelligence and IoT has birthed another worldview - the Web of Everything (IoE), where the physical and virtual domains merge consistently. In this interconnected environment, data streams universally, working with ongoing navigation and encouraging a degree of effectiveness that was once considered unfathomable.

The development of correspondence advances has been a key part in the extraordinary excursion of human progress. In 2150, correspondence rises above the limits of language and distance. Expanded Reality (AR) and Computer generated Reality (VR) have reclassified the manner in which people communicate and see their general surroundings. The once-ordinary methods of correspondence have given way to vivid encounters where actual presence is presently not an essential for significant commitment. This shift has significant ramifications for training, business, and relational connections, encouraging a worldwide town where lines disintegrate even with virtual interconnectedness.

The transformation of transportation is one more sign of the 22nd-century innovative scene. The coming of independent vehicles has changed the idea of portability, delivering conventional methods of transportation old. Urban communities are not generally gagged by gridlock, as self-driving vehicles explore flawlessly through fastidiously coordinated traffic frameworks. The skies, as well, have turned into a clamoring lane with the multiplication of flying vehicles, offering a brief look into a future where the imperatives of territory are risen above.

Energy, the backbone of modern civilization, has gone through an extreme change. The dependence on petroleum products has wound down, accounting for reasonable and sustainable wellsprings of energy. High level sunlight based innovations, tackling the force of quantum physical science, have turned into the essential wellspring of energy, giving spotless and endless capacity to a blossoming worldwide populace. The once-weakening phantom of environmental change has been relieved through an amicable mix of innovation and natural stewardship.

The medical services scene in 2150 is described by accuracy and personalization. The coming of genomics and high level diagnostics has introduced a period where clinical medicines are custom-made to individual hereditary profiles. Nanotechnology assumes a significant part in conveying designated treatments at the cell level, killing illnesses at their underlying foundations. The reconciliation of artificial intelligence in medical services facilitates finding and therapy as well as enables people to proactively deal with their prosperity through ceaseless observing and customized wellbeing plans.

The financial texture of social orders has gone through a significant change, driven by the democratization of data and the expansion of decentralized innovations. Blockchain, once inseparable from cryptographic forms of money, has developed into a fundamental innovation reshaping the shapes of administration, money, and business. Shrewd agreements, controlled by blockchain, have mechanized and smoothed out complex exchanges, disposing of the requirement for delegates and encouraging confidence in a decentralized biological system.

In the domain of schooling, the customary ideal models have been destroyed, leading to customized and versatile growth opportunities. Man-made intelligence driven instructive stages tailor educational plans to the novel learning styles and inclinations of every person, altering how information is gained and spread. Augmented reality homerooms rise above geological obstructions, empowering understudies to investigate authentic occasions, witness logical peculiarities, and participate in cooperative tasks with peers from around the globe.

The development of advanced mechanics has penetrated each area, from assembling to support ventures. Robots, furnished with cutting edge man-made consciousness and skillful mechanical abilities, team up consistently with human specialists. The once-dreaded situation of occupation uprooting has given way to a cooperative relationship where people and robots complete one another qualities, making a labor force that is more productive and creative.

The moral ramifications of mechanical headways have become progressively articulated in the 22nd hundred years. As computer based intelligence acquires phenomenal complexity and independence, inquiries of responsibility, straightforwardness, and inclination pose a potential threat. The moral structures administering the turn of events and arrangement of simulated intelligence are under steady examination, as social orders wrestle with the obligation of making innovation that is lined up with human qualities and standards.

In the midst of the mechanical wonders and cultural changes, challenges flourish. Network protection arises as a ceaseless landmark, as the interconnectivity of the computerized scene renders people and associations helpless against malevolent entertainers. Finding some kind of harmony between mechanical development and moral contemplations turns into a lasting test, requiring steady cautiousness and variation.

The development of innovation in the 22nd century is definitely not a straight movement; it is a unique exchange of leap forwards, misfortunes, and perspective changes. What's in store is definitely not a proper objective however a continuum of conceivable outcomes molded by our decisions today. As we stand at the cliff of an always unfurling future, the highlights and development of innovation coax us to explore with shrewdness, prescience, and a relentless obligation to the improvement of the human experience.

3.1 In-depth exploration of WhatsApp's key features

WhatsApp, a universal informing stage, has turned into a vital piece of day to day correspondence for millions around the world. Sent off in 2009, the application has constantly developed, presenting a plenty of highlights that reach out past basic message informing. In this extensive investigation, we dive into WhatsApp's key elements, disentangling the embroidery of its functionalities and analyzing the effect it has had on the manner in which individuals associate and impart in the 21st hundred years.

At its center, WhatsApp is an informing application that permits clients to send instant messages, interactive media records, and settle on voice and video decisions over the web. One of its characterizing highlights is its start to finish encryption, which guarantees that main the planned beneficiary can peruse the messages. This obligation to protection and security has been a foundation of WhatsApp's prosperity, cultivating trust among its client base.

Text informing, the underpinning of WhatsApp, has risen above customary SMS. Clients can send messages continuously, making a consistent and moment method of correspondence. The capacity to shape individual and gathering visits gives a flexible stage to both individual and expert discussions. Emojis and emoticons, a necessary piece of present day computerized correspondence, add a layer of articulation to messages, rising above the impediments of plain message.

Sight and sound sharing is an essential part of WhatsApp's usefulness. Clients can easily share photographs, recordings, and sound documents, improving the correspondence experience. The comfort of sharing media continuously has re-imagined the manner in which individuals share minutes, making WhatsApp a virtual collection where recollections are traded and saved.

Voice informing has arisen as a famous option in contrast to conventional text and voice calls. Clients can record and send voice messages, adding an individual touch to correspondence. This element is especially important in circumstances where composing might be unwieldy or unreasonable. The capacity to pay attention to messages whenever it might suit one upgrades the adaptability of correspondence, taking care of different client inclinations.

The presentation of voice and video calls has extended WhatsApp's collection past informing. Clients can make top notch voice and video brings over the web, killing the requirement for customary calls and working with correspondence across geological limits. This element has not just re-imagined the idea of significant distance correspondence however has additionally turned into a fundamental device for remote work and virtual gatherings.

WhatsApp Status, much the same as Stories on other web-based entertainment stages, permits clients to share fleeting updates as photographs, recordings, and text that vanish following 24 hours. This element, presented in 2017, adds a dynamic and visual aspect to WhatsApp, empowering clients to impart looks at their day to their contacts. The intelligent idea of Status, where clients can view, answer, and respond to refreshes, encourages a feeling of ongoing association.

Bunch talks have developed into a foundation of WhatsApp's social elements. Clients can make bunches for family, companions, partners, or explicit interests, encouraging a collective space for correspondence. Bunch administrators have the position to oversee participations, control settings, and guarantee the gathering's smooth working. The expansion of highlights like gathering portrayals, makes reference to, and the capacity to answer to explicit messages improves the proficiency and association of gathering correspondence.

WhatsApp Web and Work area broaden the application's arrive at past cell phones. Clients can flawlessly match up their records and proceed with discussions on a PC. This component is especially invaluable for people who invest critical energy dealing with work areas or PCs, giving a bound together informing experience across gadgets.

The approach of WhatsApp Business takes care of the requirements of ventures, private companies, and business visionaries. It offers a set-up of instruments to work with correspondence among organizations and their clients. Highlights like business profiles, computerized reactions, and the capacity to make an index of items or administrations improve the impressive skill and proficiency of business correspondence on the stage.

WhatsApp Pay, coordinated into the application in different nations, permits clients to send and get cash safely through the stage. This component takes advantage of the far and wide use of WhatsApp, changing it into a flexible instrument for correspondence as well as for monetary exchanges. The effortlessness of connecting ledgers and the commonality of the point of interaction make WhatsApp Pay an open and advantageous installment arrangement.

The steady development of WhatsApp is driven by a guarantee to development and client fulfillment. The presentation of dim mode, for example, takes care of the developing interest for interfaces that are good looking, particularly in low-light conditions. The application's versatile way to deal with client input guarantees that new highlights line up with client inclinations, improving the general client experience.

WhatsApp's prosperity isn't without its difficulties and contentions. The spread of deception and phony news through the stage has been a diligent concern. The start to finish encryption, while guaranteeing security, has additionally raised moral contemplations, as it makes it trying to screen and check the scattering of hurtful substance. WhatsApp has answered these difficulties by carrying out measures, for example, restricting message sending and teaming up with reality actually taking a look at associations to control the spread of deception.

As we explore the complicated scene of WhatsApp's elements, it is clear that the application has risen above its underlying reason as an informing stage. It has developed into a multi-layered instrument that works with correspondence, joint effort, and, surprisingly, monetary exchanges. The application's client base, crossing across different socioeconomics and geologies, bears witness to its widespread allure and utility.

The cultural effect of WhatsApp is significant. It has democratized correspondence, separating boundaries of distance and time. Families isolated by landmasses, companions scattered across urban communities, and associates working together from a distance - WhatsApp has turned into the connective tissue that ties people in the computerized age. The quickness of correspondence, the wealth of mixed media sharing, and the flexibility of the stage add to its essentialness in the regular routines of millions.

The future direction of WhatsApp is naturally attached to the advancement of innovation and the moving elements of computerized correspondence. As expanded reality, man-made consciousness, and other arising advancements keep on molding the computerized scene, WhatsApp is ready to coordinate new highlights and functionalities that line up with the developing necessities of its clients.

All in all, WhatsApp's key elements address a nuanced exchange of correspondence, network, and comfort. From its unassuming beginnings as an informing application, it has transformed into an exhaustive stage that takes special care of different parts of present day life.

As we cross the computerized outskirts, WhatsApp remains as a demonstration of the groundbreaking force of innovation in cultivating significant associations and reshaping the manner in which we convey in an undeniably interconnected world.

3.2 The evolution of the platform over time

The development of any stage is a powerful story, a complicated story woven by the interaction of advancement, client input, and the determined quest for greatness. In following the direction of a stage's development over the long run, one not just finds the achievements that imprint its process yet in addition acquires understanding into the more extensive mechanical and cultural movements that have formed its turn of events. This investigation is especially piercing when applied to stages that have become necessary to the texture of our computerized presence.

Think about the advancement of web-based entertainment monster Facebook, sent off in 2004 by Imprint Zuckerberg and his school flat mates. In its early stages, Facebook was an unassuming systems administration stage, bound to the limits of Harvard College. Its essential capability was to interface understudies inside the college, permitting them to make profiles, share refreshes, and convey inside a shut local area. The stage's development from a grounds explicit organization to a worldwide online entertainment behemoth is a demonstration of its flexibility and the versatility of its fundamental engineering.

As Facebook extended its client base past Harvard, it went through a progression of extraordinary stages. The presentation of the News channel in 2006 denoted a change in outlook, totaling refreshes from companions and pages into a brought together stream. This element modified the client experience as well as established the groundwork for a more vivid and drawing in stage. The ensuing expansion of the Like button in 2009 acquainted another aspect with client collaborations, giving a straightforward yet strong method for communicating appreciation and commitment.

The advancement of Facebook's point of interaction reflects more extensive plan patterns and client assumptions. Throughout the long term, the stage has gone through various overhauls, changing from a text-weighty point of interaction to an outwardly determined format. The presentation of cover photographs, extended sight and sound sharing capacities, and the accentuation on visual substance all add to a more unique and intuitive client experience. These plan decisions take care of developing stylish inclinations as well as line up with the rising accentuation on visual narrating in the advanced age.

The combination of outsider applications and games into the Facebook environment extended its usefulness, transforming it into a diverse stage. FarmVille, for example, turned into a social peculiarity, delineating the potential for social gaming inside the Facebook climate. This introduction to social gaming laid the preparation for the gamification of social communications, with clients participating in well disposed rivalries and joint efforts inside the stage.

The presentation of Facebook Pages in 2007 denoted an essential second in the stage's development, broadening its arrive at past individual profiles to envelop organizations, famous people, and associations. Brands could now lay out a computerized presence, interfacing with their crowd in a more organized and versatile way. The ensuing presentation of elements like Experiences furnished page directors with significant investigation, enabling them to comprehend and upgrade their computerized procedures.

The versatile unrest significantly affected Facebook's advancement. The send off of the Facebook portable application in 2010 worked with in a hurry access, untethering clients from work areas and PCs. The stage's variation to cell phones mirrored a more extensive industry pattern, where clients progressively consumed content on cell phones and tablets. The securing of Instagram in 2012 and WhatsApp in 2014 further set Facebook's portable driven procedure, coordinating famous stages that took special care of visual substance and texting.

The Live Video highlight, presented in 2016, addressed a change in perspective in satisfied creation and utilization. Clients could now communicate real time recordings, encouraging ongoing cooperations with their crowd. This component not just exploited the developing prominence of video content yet in addition lined up with the business wide shift towards live and legitimate encounters in the computerized domain. The ensuing presentation of Stories in 2017 further supported this pattern, offering a fleeting and vivid organization for content sharing.

In any case, Facebook's advancement has not been without its difficulties and discussions. The stage's job in the spread of phony news and the abuse of client information for designated promoting started far reaching examination and calls for expanded guideline. The Cambridge Analytica outrage in 2018, where individual information of millions of clients was gathered without assent, turned into a turning point, provoking a reexamination of protection rehearses inside the stage.

In light of these difficulties, Facebook has embraced a progression of measures to improve client protection and security. The execution of GDPR-consistent information controls, the acquaintance of devices with oversee promotion inclinations, and the accentuation on start to finish encryption in informing administrations mirror a purposeful work to address client concerns and line up with developing security guidelines.

The advancing scene of online entertainment and computerized correspondence likewise affected Facebook's essential acquisitions. Oculus, procured in 2014, situated Facebook in the blossoming field of computer generated reality. The investigation of computer generated reality spaces and the joining of VR advancements into the stage foretell a future where social collaborations rise above topographical limitations, drenching clients in shared computerized conditions.

The advancement of Facebook is meaningful of the more extensive patterns in the tech business. The shift towards portable first encounters, the accentuation on visual substance, and the coordination of expanded and augmented reality all reverberation the direction of computerized advancement. The stage's reaction to cultural worries around protection and falsehood mirrors the developing familiarity with moral contemplations in the turn of events and arrangement of advanced advancements.

Looking forward, the direction of Facebook's advancement remains naturally attached to the always changing scene of innovation and client assumptions. The investigation of arising advancements like man-made reasoning, increased reality, and the metaverse highlights Facebook's obligation to remaining at the very front of development. The quest for making a more associated and vivid computerized experience recommends that the stage will keep on developing, adjusting to the moving tides of the advanced period.

All in all, the development of a stage like Facebook is an embroidery woven with strings of development, transformation, and reaction to cultural elements. From its modest starting points as a college organizing device to its ongoing status as a worldwide online entertainment monster, Facebook's process mirrors the more extensive story of the computerized age. The stage's capacity to explore difficulties, embrace new advancements, and answer client needs positions it as a unique player in the continuous adventure of mechanical development. As we glance back at its set of experiences, we gain not just a review on the development of a solitary stage yet additionally a nuanced comprehension of the more extensive powers that shape the computerized scene we occupy today.

3.3 User feedback and how it shaped feature development

In the perplexing dance between innovation makers and clients, the trading of criticism is a significant power forming the development of computerized stages. Client input fills in as a compass, directing engineers through the consistently changing scene of client assumptions, inclinations, and requirements. This harmonious connection among clients and stage designers is especially obvious in the ceaseless refinement and extension of elements. In this investigation, we dig into the significant effect of client criticism on highlight advancement, analyzing how it has shaped the computerized scene and raised client encounters.

At the core of the client input circle is a unique discussion that rises above customary thoughts of item improvement. Stages, going from virtual entertainment goliaths to efficiency instruments and portable applications, are not static substances but rather living environments that answer the assorted voices of their client base. The advancement of elements is a demonstration of the responsiveness of engineers to the nuanced signals given by clients exploring the computerized domain.

Think about the domain of virtual entertainment stages, where the crossing point of human association and advanced points of interaction is generally articulated. Facebook, one of the trailblazers in the web-based entertainment scene, has gone through a heap of element improvements molded by client criticism. The presentation of the Like button, for example, was an immediate reaction to the client's craving for a speedy and expressive method for interfacing with posts. Which began as a straightforward thumbs-up has turned into an omnipresent image of endorsement and commitment, showing how a little element can resound significantly with client assumptions.

The extension of Facebook's response buttons, permitting clients to communicate a range of feelings past preferring a post, is another example where client input has driven include improvement. Clients looked for a more nuanced method for answering substance, and Facebook answered by giving a range of responses - love, haha, goodness, miserable, and irate. This advancement improved the stage's expressive abilities as well as recognized the variety of client feelings.

The iterative improvement of Facebook's protection settings is a demonstration of the stage's responsiveness to client concerns. As clients turned out to be progressively aware of their advanced impression and the likely ramifications of oversharing, Facebook presented more granular powers over protection settings. Clients could now modify the perceivability of their posts, oversee companion records, and control who could label them in photographs. These changes were not erratic choices made in segregation; they were reactions to the developing assumptions and awarenesses of the client local area.

Twitter, another unmistakable web-based entertainment stage, has additionally been molded by client criticism in its element advancement. As far as possible for tweets, initially set at 140 characters, was a central trait of the stage. In any case, client criticism demonstrated a craving for more extensive articulation. Accordingly, Twitter multiplied as far as possible to 280, a move that earned blended responses however mirrored the stage's obligation to adjusting to client needs.

The presentation of Twitter strings, permitting clients to string together a progression of tweets, is one more illustration of element improvement informed by client conduct. Clients were at that point utilizing whimsical strategies, like numbering tweets, to make strings. Perceiving this, Twitter formalized the interaction, giving a consistent and organized way for clients to share broadened considerations or stories.

Instagram, a stage inseparable from visual narrating, has gone through groundbreaking element improvement in light of client criticism. The presentation of Instagram Stories was an immediate reaction to the progress of a comparable element on Snapchat.

Clients looked for a more vaporous and unconstrained method for sharing minutes, and Instagram coordinated Stories into its foundation. The progress of this element exhibited the stage's versatility as well as displayed the force of noticing and answering client conduct across various applications.

Instagram's accentuation on visual substance normally prompted the advancement of its photograph and video altering instruments. Channels, when an original expansion, turned into a staple of the stage, empowering clients to upgrade and redo their visual stories. The ensuing presentation of further developed altering highlights, for example, the capacity to change splendor, difference, and immersion, was an immediate reaction clients hoping for more prominent inventive control.

The IGTV include on Instagram, a stage for longer-structure video content, arose as a reaction to the developing fame of video content across web-based entertainment. Clients were progressively captivating with recordings, and Instagram answered by making a devoted space for upward, long-structure recordings inside the application. This represents how highlight improvement can be an essential reaction to more extensive patterns in client conduct.

Past virtual entertainment, efficiency instruments and applications have additionally advanced through the iterative course of client input. Microsoft Office 365, a thorough set-up of efficiency instruments, has a client criticism component coordinated into its point of interaction. Clients can propose new highlights, report issues, and decision on the ideas of others. This immediate channel for client input engages the client local area to partake in the stage's development effectively.

The cooperative idea of Google Docs, where various clients can all the while alter a report progressively, is a component that rose up out of client input. The craving for consistent joint effort and the disposal of rendition control issues incited Google to foster a record altering stage that reflected the elements of continuous cooperation. Google Docs, alongside Sheets and Slides, addresses a change in perspective in co-operative efficiency, driven by client requirements and assumptions.

Portable applications, at the front of the advanced insight, are molded by client criticism as they continued looking for easy to use interfaces and consistent usefulness. The development of ride-sharing applications like Uber and Lyft is a great representation. The presentation of highlights like ongoing following, forthright evaluating, and driver evaluations mirrors a sharp responsiveness to client inclinations and concerns.

Language learning applications, like Duolingo, have bridled client input to refine their way to deal with language obtaining. Gamification components, where clients acquire focuses and prizes for finishing examples, were presented in view of the perception that clients answered decidedly to intuitive and game-like highlights.

The persistent refinement of language courses in light of client execution information is a demonstration of the stage's obligation to customized and successful opportunities for growth.

The effect of client input stretches out past individual highlights to the actual pith of stage personality. Consider the development of the video-sharing stage YouTube. The stage's choice to embrace and adapt client produced content through the YouTube Accomplice Program was impacted by client conduct. As happy makers ran to the stage, producing a different cluster of recordings, YouTube answered by giving a system to makers to adapt their substance through notices and sponsorships.

The algorithmic proposals on YouTube, which recommend recordings in light of a client's review history, commitment examples, and inclinations, are an immediate reaction to the's comprehension stage might interpret client conduct. The objective isn't simply to give content yet to organize a customized and drawing in experience for every client, molding the stage into a unique substance disclosure motor.

Be that as it may, the harmonious connection among clients and stage engineers isn't without its intricacies. The democratization of input through online entertainment has enabled clients to voice their perspectives, reactions, and ideas straightforwardly to stage makers. While this immediate line of correspondence can prompt positive turns of events, it likewise opens stages to a downpour of suppositions that shift generally in legitimacy and pertinence.

The test for stage designers is to filter through this racket of voices, knowing important bits of knowledge from commotion. The presentation of highlights like studies, surveys, and beta testing programs assists stages with social affair organized and noteworthy criticism. These systems permit designers to focus on include improvements in light of the aggregate necessities and wants of their client base.

The iterative idea of component improvement is an impression of the light-footed systems embraced by numerous tech organizations. The capacity to deliver least practical items, assemble client input, and iteratively refine highlights is a sign of this methodology. It permits engineers to test speculations, adjust to changing client elements, and keep away from the traps of concentrating on highlights that may not reverberate with clients.

Past the domain of virtual entertainment and efficiency instruments, gaming stages offer a remarkable point of view because of client input on include improvement. The iterative arrival of patches, refreshes, and downloadable substance (DLC) in the gaming business mirrors a pledge to answering player criticism. Game designers effectively draw in with online networks, gatherings, and virtual entertainment to check player feeling and address issues going from bugs and errors to ongoing interaction mechanics.

The idea of early access, where games are delivered to the general population in an incomplete state, is a striking sign of this methodology. Engineers influence player criticism to shape the last form of the game, including the local area in the co-making of the gaming experience. This iterative model takes into consideration consistent refinement and guarantees that the eventual outcome adjusts all the more intimately with player assumptions.

Client criticism isn't restricted to responsive changes; it likewise assumes a vital part in forming the essential course of stages. The outcome of crowdfunding stages like Kickstarter and Indiegogo relies on the dynamic support and criticism of patrons. Projects that reverberate with benefactors get subsidizing, while those that neglect to catch interest might have to reconsider their methodology in light of client criticism and inclinations.

In the realm of online business, stages like Amazon have utilized client surveys and evaluations as a focal component of their plan of action. Client input on items shapes buying choices for different clients, making an upright cycle where quality items get positive surveys, driving more deals. This framework enables clients to go with informed decisions as well as boosts merchants to keep up with excellent guidelines.

The development of route applications like Google Guides is a demonstration of the combination of client criticism continuously route. Clients can report issues like gridlock, mishaps, and street terminations straightforwardly through the application. This publicly supported information not just guides individual clients in arranging their courses yet in addition adds to the general precision and responsiveness of the route framework.

The cooperative idea of open-source projects addresses an outrageous type of client contribution in highlight advancement. Stages like Linux, Apache, and Mozilla Firefox blossom with the aggregate commitments and criticism of a worldwide local area of designers. The development of open-source programming is a majority rule process where clients effectively shape the course and usefulness of the stage through their code commitments and ideas.

As we explore the immense scope of computerized stages, it becomes clear that client criticism is certainly not an inactive element however a functioning power controlling the boat of innovative advancement. It is a discourse, a persistent trade that changes computerized stages from static devices into dynamic biological systems. The democratization of criticism enables clients to be shoppers as well as dynamic members in the co-formation of the advanced scene.

However, the connection among clients and stages isn't absent any and all strains. The harmony between answering client criticism and keeping an intelligible and vital vision represents a ceaseless test. Client inclinations can be different and now and again clashing, expecting engineers to pursue choices that line up with the all-encompassing objectives of the stage while regarding the requirements of their client local area.

The job of client input stretches out past individual highlights to general subjects of stage morals and administration. As stages become focal courses of data and correspondence, issues of content control, deception, and client wellbeing arise as basic worries. The criticism circle presently incorporates contemplations of mindful computer based intelligence, algorithmic predispositions, and the moral ramifications of stage plan.

The Cambridge Analytica outrage that shook Facebook in 2018 highlighted the significance of moral contemplations in include advancement. The unapproved gathering of client information for political purposes incited a retribution inside the tech business in regards to the capable treatment of client data. Accordingly, stages have been constrained to return to their information protection arrangements, upgrade safety efforts, and participate in more straightforward correspondence with clients about the utilization of their information.

As we peer into the future, the job of client criticism in molding elements will keep on advancing. The combination of man-made brainpower and AI into stages acquaints new aspects with client collaborations. Prescient examination, customized suggestions, and versatile connection points are regions where client criticism will assume a vital part in refining calculations and guaranteeing that computer based intelligence driven highlights line up with client assumptions.

The idea of the metaverse, an interconnected computer generated experience space, presents a worldview where client criticism might shape highlights as well as whole advanced environments. As clients explore vivid advanced conditions, their inclinations, ways of behaving, and communications will give significant information to forming the development of the metaverse. The difficulties of protection, security, and moral contemplations in the metaverse will require an elevated dependence on client criticism to find some kind of harmony.

All in all, the cooperative connection among clients and stage designers is a foundation of the computerized age. The advancement of elements is certainly not a road that goes only one direction however a persistent discourse where clients and designers participate in a powerful trade of thoughts, inclinations, and evaluates. The iterative idea of component improvement mirrors a guarantee to responsiveness, versatility, and the client driven ethos that characterizes fruitful computerized stages.

As stages proceed to develop and push the limits of innovation, the centrality of client criticism will just escalate. The democratization of criticism channels, the hug of spry systems, and the mix of client input into vital dynamic all add to a computerized scene where clients are buyers as well as co-makers. In this continuous dance among makers and clients, the development of highlights turns into an impression of the aggregate yearnings, values, and dreams that shape the computerized future we by and large explore

Chapter 4

User-Friendly Interface

In the quickly developing scene of innovation, an easy to understand interface has turned into a principal part of programming plan. As the advanced domain proceeds to extend and coordinate into each feature of our lives, the significance of making points of interaction that are instinctive, effective, and available couldn't possibly be more significant. An easy to understand connection point isn't simply a plan component; a passage works with the cooperation among people and machines, cultivating a consistent and charming client experience.

At its center, an easy to use connection point is described by its capacity to take special care of the different necessities and assumptions for clients, no matter what their specialized capability. This inclusivity is fundamental in our current reality where advanced proficiency shifts broadly, and programming applications are utilized by people across various age gatherings, foundations, and expertise levels. The test lies in making a connection point that isn't just outwardly engaging yet in addition practical, giving a liquid route experience that obliges the two learners and prepared clients.

One of the essential standards of an easy to understand point of interaction is straightforwardness. The plan ought to focus on lucidity and straightforwardness, limiting pointless intricacy. At the point when clients communicate with a product application, they ought to have the option to comprehend its functionalities and elements easily. This effortlessness reaches out past visual feel to the basic engineering of the connection point, guaranteeing that the client venture is smoothed out and sensible.

Viable route is a foundation of easy to understand plan. Clients ought to have the option to cross the connection point effortlessly, finding the data or playing out the activities they want without superfluous obstacles. Natural route improves the general client experience, diminishing disappointment and expanding proficiency. Insightful position of menus, buttons, and intuitive components adds to the formation of a route framework that feels natural, directing clients through the connection point consistently.

Visual components assume a vital part in laying out an easy to use interface. The utilization of clear, succinct, and steady plan components adds to the general ease of use of the application. Consistency in plan cultivates a feeling of commonality, empowering clients to foresee the area and conduct of components all through the connection point. This consistency is a vital consider building client trust and certainty, as clients can depend on their earlier information while connecting with various pieces of the product.

Notwithstanding visual lucidity, an easy to use point of interaction ought to focus on openness. Openness goes past taking special care of clients with incapacities; it includes planning for a different client base with shifting necessities and inclinations. This incorporates contemplations for variety contrast, text dimension, and elective route techniques. By embracing availability standards, creators can make interfaces that are easy to understand for the larger part as well as accommodating of people with explicit necessities.

Input components are basic to an easy to understand interface. Clients ought to get clear and convenient input on their activities inside the application. Whether it's clicking a button, presenting a structure, or starting a cycle, input guarantees clients that their activities have been perceived and are advancing as planned. Obvious prompts, for example, stacking pointers or achievement messages, add to a feeling of responsiveness and keep clients educated about the status regarding their cooperations.

Easy to understand points of interaction ought to likewise be versatile to various gadgets and screen sizes. In the time of portable figuring, responsive plan is essential. Applications need to flawlessly change between work areas, tablets, and cell phones, giving a steady and enhanced insight across different stages. This flexibility isn't just a specialized prerequisite yet in addition an impression of the client driven approach, recognizing the shifted ways people draw in with computerized content.

The language utilized inside the connection point is one more basic part of ease of use. The text ought to be compact, language free, and straightforward. Clear and direct language upgrades client understanding and diminishes the gamble of disarray or error. The objective is to impart data in a way that reverberates with the interest group, regardless of their knowledge of specialized phrasing.

Easy to understand connection points are not static substances; they ought to develop in light of client criticism and changing mechanical scenes. Consistent improvement is vital to guaranteeing that the connection point stays important and compelling over the long run. Ordinary convenience testing, criticism assortment, and cycle are fundamental parts of the plan interaction. This iterative methodology permits architects to refine and improve the connection point in view of genuine client encounters and inclinations.

With regards to programming improvement, the idea of easy to understand interfaces reaches out past independent applications to incorporate the combination of frameworks and interoperability between various programming items. A consistent progression of data between interconnected applications adds to a comprehensive client experience. For instance, the reconciliation of outsider modules or joint effort devices ought to be executed such that supplements the general point of interaction, as opposed to presenting intricacy or irregularities.

The development of easy to understand interfaces has been intently attached to headways in human-PC collaboration. From order line connection points to graphical UIs (GUIs) and contact based interfaces, every movement has intended to make innovation more available and client driven. The ascent of voice-controlled connection points and signal based cooperations addresses the continuous mission for interfaces that line up with normal human ways of behaving, further limiting the expectation to absorb information for clients.

In the domain of website composition, the standards of easy to understand connection points are especially articulated. Sites act as computerized customer facing facades, data centers, and intelligent stages, requiring an elevated spotlight on client experience. Quick stacking times, responsive designs, and instinctive route are principal for holding guests and empowering delayed commitment. The client's excursion through a site ought to be a liquid and pleasant experience, from the underlying presentation page to the finish of wanted activities.

Web based business stages, specifically, represent the meaning of easy to use interfaces. The web based shopping experience relies on the client's capacity to easily peruse items, add things to the truck, and complete exchanges. A very much planned web based business interface expects client needs, gives pertinent data, and improves on the buying system. Security and straightforwardness in monetary exchanges likewise add to client certainty, encouraging a positive connection between the client and the stage.

With regards to portable applications, easy to use connection points are instrumental in guaranteeing the achievement and broad reception of the application. Versatile clients, frequently in a hurry and with restricted capacities to focus, require interfaces that are succinct, productive, and outwardly captivating. Versatile application configuration ought to focus on the most fundamental highlights, introducing them in an easy to understand way that lines up with the constraints and qualities of cell phones.

Virtual entertainment stages embody the inescapable impact of easy to understand interfaces on client commitment. The outcome of stages like Facebook, Instagram, and Twitter is ascribed not exclusively to their substance yet in addition to the plan of the connection points that energize client collaboration and investigation. Elements like the timetable, notices, and sharing choices are introduced in a way that supports client cooperation, changing these stages into dynamic center points of social movement.

The job of client experience (UX) plan in creating easy to understand interfaces couldn't possibly be more significant. UX planners dive into the brain science of client conduct, concentrating on how people associate with advanced frameworks and recognizing problem areas and open doors for development. Through strategies, for example, client personas, venture planning, and wireframing, UX creators make a diagram for an easy to use interface that lines up with client assumptions and objectives.

As innovation keeps on progressing, arising patterns shape the scene of easy to understand interfaces. Expanded reality (AR) and computer generated reality (VR) interfaces present new difficulties and open doors for originators. The spatial and vivid nature of these connection points requires a reconsidering of conventional plan standards, zeroing in on how clients explore and collaborate inside virtual conditions. The combination of physical and advanced domains in expanded reality opens up creative opportunities for easy to understand interfaces in different spaces, from gaming to training and then some.

Man-made brainpower (computer based intelligence) is another groundbreaking power affecting easy to understand interfaces. AI calculations can break down client conduct, inclinations, and examples to powerfully customize the connection point. From prescribing content to foreseeing client activities, man-made intelligence adds to a more customized and client driven insight. Be that as it may, the moral ramifications of man-made intelligence driven interfaces, including issues connected with protection and predisposition, highlight the significance of capable and straightforward plan rehearses.

All in all, the advancement of easy to use connection points is entwined with the more extensive account of mechanical advancement. From the beginning of figuring to the time of vivid innovations, the journey for interfaces that focus on the client experience has been a steady. Straightforwardness, lucidity, versatility, and inclusivity are the core values that support easy to understand plan. As innovation keeps on propelling, the job of design.

4.1 Analysis of WhatsApp's user interface design

WhatsApp, a universally pervasive informing application, has turned into a vital piece of current correspondence, associating people across the world continuously. As we dive into an examination of WhatsApp's UI (UI) plan, it is fundamental to perceive the significant effect this stage has had on forming how individuals impart. The plan decisions made by WhatsApp play had a critical impact in its far and wide reception and proceeded with client commitment.

One of the champion elements of WhatsApp's UI configuration is its effortlessness. The point of interaction is perfect and cleaned up, giving clients a clear informing stage that focuses on usefulness. The home screen, the focal center of client action, includes a rundown of progressing discussions in a sequential request, giving speedy admittance to ongoing collaborations. This straightforwardness in format lines up with the guideline of limiting mental burden, permitting clients to zero in on their discussions without interruptions.

The visit interface itself is intended for usability. The discussion bubbles are obviously depicted, with approaching messages on the left and active messages on the right. This visual differentiation supports rapidly distinguishing the shipper and recipient of each message, adding to a consistent and natural discussion stream.

The utilization of various varieties for every member further improves clearness, making it simple for clients to follow the movement of the discussion.

WhatsApp's choice to embrace a green variety plot all through its UI adds to the stage's visual character. The decision of green isn't just particular yet additionally lines up with the brand's relationship with correspondence and availability. Green has implications of energy, development, and concordance, establishing an outwardly satisfying climate for clients. The reliable utilization of variety across the application cultivates a feeling of union and builds up the memorability's.

The incorporation of media components inside the talk point of interaction is one more significant part of WhatsApp's plan. Clients can flawlessly share pictures, recordings, reports, and sound messages inside the visit string. The joining of interactive media adds lavishness to the correspondence experience, permitting clients to convey a different scope of content past text. The UI guarantees that mixed media components are shown in an easy to use way, with see thumbnails and natural controls for playback or review.

The fuse of voice informing as an essential capabilities WhatsApp separated in the informing application scene. The UI for voice informing is planned considering effortlessness and availability. Clients can record and send voice messages with a solitary tap, killing the requirement for composing. The visual portrayal of voice messages, with waveform movements demonstrating sound force, adds a dynamic and drawing in component to the UI. This element takes special care of clients who favor vocal correspondence, adding to the stage's adaptability.

WhatsApp's way to deal with bunch visits is one more part of its UI plan that warrants examination. Bunch visits unite numerous clients in a solitary discussion string, cultivating cooperation and local area. The UI capably deals with the intricacy of gathering communications by showing member names and profile pictures, giving a visual outline of the discussion's benefactors. The capacity to redo social scenes, including notices and protection choices, adds a layer of personalization, engaging clients to fit their gathering talk insight to their inclinations.

The reconciliation of start to finish encryption as a basic security highlight is a plan decision that mirrors WhatsApp's obligation to client protection. While encryption itself is a specialized viewpoint, its portrayal in the UI is urgent. WhatsApp imparts the security status of discussions through viewable signs, like the utilization of lock symbols and variety markers. This straightforwardness enables clients with data about the security of their messages, cultivating trust in the stage.

The status highlight, permitting clients to share refreshes as text, photographs, or recordings that vanish following 24 hours, acquaints a unique component with WhatsApp's UI. The plan of the status highlight is natural, with a noticeable situation on the home screen.

Clients can without much of a stretch view and answer the situations with their contacts, making a feeling of ongoing association. The fleeting idea of notices lines up with the more extensive pattern of transient substance in virtual entertainment, giving a space to relaxed and unconstrained sharing.

WhatsApp's fuse of voice and video calling inside the application broadens the correspondence abilities past text. The UI for calling is consistently coordinated into the visit interface, with devoted buttons for starting voice or video calls. The plan guarantees that settling on a decision is a direct interaction, with choices to switch among front and back cameras during video calls and quiet/unmute sound. The visual portrayal of progressing calls, with contact names and call term, adds a layer of straightforwardness to the client experience.

The contact the board framework inside WhatsApp is intended to work with simple association with companions, family, and partners. Clients can add contacts by adjusting their telephone's location book or by straightforwardly entering contact data. The UI for overseeing contacts is natural, with choices to see ongoing talks, start new discussions, or access contact subtleties. The utilization of profile pictures improves the visual ID of contacts, adding to a more customized and client driven insight.

Warnings are a basic part of any informing application, and WhatsApp's UI configuration gives cautious consideration to this component. The stage gives clients granular command over notice inclinations, permitting them to modify cautions for messages, calls, and gathering movement. The utilization of warning identifications on the application symbol keeps clients informed about uninitiated messages, making an obvious prompt for commitment. The UI guarantees that warnings are inconspicuous yet enlightening, finding some kind of harmony between keeping clients associated and regarding their craving for security.

WhatsApp Web, the work area expansion of the portable application, addresses a smart expansion of the stage's UI plan. The work area interface reflects the portable UI, making a steady encounter for clients changing between gadgets. The plan guarantees that the functionalities stay in one piece, including the capacity to send messages, share media, and partake in calls. The QR code-based verification for WhatsApp Web rearranges the login cycle, keeping up with the security of client accounts.

As we ponder WhatsApp's UI plan, recognizing the development of the stage after some time is fundamental. The presentation of elements like stickers, energized emoticons, and the capacity to cite messages in answers mirrors a pledge to remaining important and connecting with for clients. The iterative idea of UI refreshes, driven by client input and innovative progressions, guarantees that WhatsApp stays a contemporary and client driven correspondence stage.

Be that as it may, it isn't without its reactions. The regular updates and changes to the UI, while expecting to upgrade the client experience, can in some cases lead to client disarray and an expectation to learn and adapt. Clients acquainted with a specific design might find it trying to adjust to visit changes, stressing the fragile harmony among development and client commonality.

All in all, WhatsApp's UI configuration remains as a demonstration of the force of straightforwardness, usefulness, and client centricity in making a worldwide took on informing stage. The spotless and natural plan, combined with a rich arrangement of highlights, has added to WhatsApp's conspicuousness in the domain of computerized correspondence. As innovation proceeds to progress, and client assumptions develop, WhatsApp's obligation to refining its UI will assume a vital part in keeping up with its situation as a main correspondence stage. The examination of WhatsApp's UI configuration fills in as an important investigation of the standards and contemplations that support fruitful UI plan with regards to a broadly utilized informing application.

4.2 The role of simplicity in attracting a diverse user base

Straightforwardness, frequently thought to be an ethicalness in different parts of life, holds an especially critical job in the domain of UI plan. In the powerful scene of innovation, where items and administrations take special care of a different crowd with shifting degrees of specialized skill, effortlessness arises as a vital figure drawing in and holding clients. This examination dives into the multi-layered job of effortlessness in UI configuration, investigating how a clear and straightforward plan approach cultivates inclusivity, openness, and far and wide client reception.

At the center of straightforwardness in UI configuration is the standard of decreasing intricacy. A basic connection point is one that presents data and functionalities in a reasonable, unambiguous way, limiting mental burden for clients. This approach recognizes that clients come from different foundations, with shifting degrees of knowledge of innovation, and looks to establish a climate that is instinctive and simple to explore.

The primary layer of straightforwardness is apparent in the visual plan of UIs. Jumbled and excessively complex points of interaction can overpower clients, prompting disarray and dissatisfaction. A straightforward plan, then again, utilizes a spotless format, sensible utilization of blank area, and a restricted variety range, establishing an outwardly engaging and cleaned up climate. This visual effortlessness upgrades the tasteful allure as well as adds to the client's capacity to zero in on the fundamental components of the connection point.

The idea of straightforwardness reaches out to the route design of a connection point. A very much planned route framework guarantees that clients can undoubtedly find what they are searching for without becoming mixed up in a maze of menus and choices.

Straightforward route includes a consistent pecking order, clear names, and instinctive situation of intelligent components. Clients ought to have the option to anticipate where to track down unambiguous elements, diminishing the requirement for broad investigation and experimentation collaborations.

With regards to drawing in a different client base, straightforwardness turns into a binding together variable that scaffolds holes in computerized education and mechanical capability. Clients going from fledglings to specialists ought to have the option to communicate with the point of interaction without feeling overpowered or rejected. For people less acquainted with innovation, a basic point of interaction goes about as an inviting section point, diminishing the boundaries to reception and empowering investigation.

Think about the case of cell phones. The straightforwardness of cell phone interfaces plays had a crucial impact in their far and wide reception across age gatherings and socioeconomics. The application symbols, contact motions, and generally speaking format of versatile points of interaction are planned effortlessly of purpose. This straightforwardness has engaged people, independent of their age or innovative foundation, to consistently incorporate cell phones into their day to day routines.

Straightforwardness additionally converges with availability, guaranteeing that points of interaction are usable by people with assorted capacities and requirements. Clear and succinct plan components, alongside instinctive route, add to a more comprehensive client experience. Availability highlights, for example, customizable text sizes, high differentiation modes, and screen peruser similarity, improve the ease of use of points of interaction for people with visual weaknesses or different inabilities.

In addition, straightforwardness in plan lines up with the standards of widespread plan, which advocates for establishing items and conditions that are usable by individuals of all capacities, ages, and foundations. A generally planned interface obliges a wide range of clients, perceiving that variety stretches out past innovative capability to incorporate variables like language, social contrasts, and actual capacities.

Language assumes a vital part in working on the client experience. The selection of words, expressions, and guidelines inside a connection point ought to be clear, compact, and without any trace of superfluous language. A basic and direct language supports understanding as well as works with a more comprehensive encounter for clients with fluctuating degrees of language capability.

Think about the worldwide reach of advanced items and administrations. Straightforwardness in language is fundamental while taking special care of a different, multicultural client base. By keeping away from excessively specialized terms and utilizing plain language, architects can make interfaces that resound with clients from various semantic foundations.

This etymological straightforwardness stretches out to blunder messages, tooltips, and educational message, guaranteeing that clients can comprehend and follow up on the data introduced.

Chasing effortlessness, architects frequently influence the force of iconography. Symbols, when planned mindfully, can convey importance in a minimized and generally justifiable manner. Straightforward and natural symbols act as viewable signs, helping clients in rapidly getting a handle on the motivation behind different elements or activities. In any case, it is vital to work out some kind of harmony, as excessively dynamic or uncertain symbols can prompt disarray.

Besides, the job of effortlessness is amplified with regards to onboarding - the underlying experience clients have with an application or stage. The onboarding system ought to be clear, directing clients through the fundamental highlights and functionalities. A straightforward onboarding experience establishes the vibe for client communication, assisting people with getting to know the point of interaction and lessening the gamble of relinquishment because of intricacy.

Straightforwardness reaches out past the visual and navigational perspectives to the presentation of a point of interaction. A basic and responsive connection point adds to a positive client experience. Slow burden times, inert controls, or over the top activitys can sabotage the effortlessness of configuration, prompting client dissatisfaction. Execution streamlining is a necessary piece of effortlessness, guaranteeing that clients can collaborate with the connection point without a hitch and without delays.

In the domain of online business, effortlessness is a basic consider driving change. The client venture, from item revelation to checkout, ought to be smoothed out and natural. Perplexing and tangled checkout cycles can bring about deserted trucks and lost deals. Web based business stages that focus on straightforwardness in the perusing and buying experience will generally draw in and hold a more different client base, incorporating people with shifting degrees of internet shopping mastery.

Straightforwardness is additionally interlaced with the idea of data design - the association and construction of content inside a point of interaction. An efficient data design guarantees that clients can rapidly find the data they need. Straightforward arrangement, clear naming, and legitimate gathering of content add to a point of interaction that is easy to understand and obliging to assorted data looking for ways of behaving.

Think about the job of straightforwardness in virtual entertainment stages. The progress of stages like Facebook and Twitter lies in their capacity to distil complex social collaborations into a straightforward and natural connection point. Clients can undoubtedly post refreshes, share content, and draw in with others without exploring through layers of intricacy.

This straightforwardness has been a main impetus in the broad reception of online entertainment across different socioeconomics.

With regards to programming applications, the job of straightforwardness stretches out to the customization choices accessible to clients. While customization is a significant element, an overabundance of choices can overpower clients. Straightforwardness in customization includes offering a reasonable arrangement of choices, introduced in an unmistakable and justifiable way. This approach guarantees that clients can customize their experience without being impeded by a wealth of decisions.

The plan reasoning of moderation adjusts intimately with the idea of effortlessness. Moderate plan intends to pass significance on using insignificant components -

decreasing the plan to its fundamental parts. This approach embraces straightforwardness in both structure and capability, making connection points that are outwardly exquisite and practically effective. The moderate ethos reverberates with clients who value a spotless and cleaned up tasteful.

Nonetheless, accomplishing straightforwardness isn't inseparable from eliminating highlights or forfeiting usefulness. A straightforward connection point can in any case offer a rich arrangement of elements, given that they are introduced in a coordinated and easy to use way. The test lies in finding some kind of harmony - conveying the essential usefulness without overpowering clients with superfluous intricacy.

In the space of efficiency apparatuses, straightforwardness is essential for upgrading client concentration and proficiency. Applications like note-taking instruments, project the board stages, and cooperation programming benefit from a basic and natural plan. Clients ought to have the option to perform errands, coordinate data, and team up consistently, without being impeded by a lofty expectation to learn and adapt.

The coming of versatile applications has highlighted the meaning of straightforwardness in plan. Portable connection points, obliged by more modest screens and contact based communications, require an engaged and smoothed out approach. Effective versatile applications focus on straightforwardness in design, route, and connection, perceiving that clients frequently draw in with these applications in a hurry and in circumstances where speedy and natural communications are vital.

Additionally, the job of straightforwardness is emphasizd in arising advances like expanded reality (AR) and computer generated reality (VR). These vivid conditions request interfaces that are outwardly engaging as well as natural in a three-layered space. The test lies in improving on cooperations without forfeiting the lavishness of the vivid experience. Basic and instinctive signals, alongside moderate plan components, add to a more open and charming AR/VR interface.

As innovation keeps on propelling, the job of effortlessness in UI configuration stays a core value. The coming of voice-controlled interfaces, man-made brainpower, and the Web of Things (IoT) presents new difficulties and open doors for originators. Straightforwardness in these settings includes making connection points that influence cutting edge innovations while guaranteeing that the collaborations stay normal, easy to use, and without superfluous intricacy.

All in all, the job of effortlessness in drawing in a different client base couldn't possibly be more significant. Straightforwardness fills in as a bringing together power that rises above contrasts in mechanical capability, social foundations, and individual inclinations. A straightforward connection point encourages inclusivity, making computerized items and administrations open to an expansive crowd. Whether in the domain of portable applications, web based business stages, online entertainment, or arising innovations, effortlessness stays a foundation of effective UI plan. As creators explore the consistently advancing scene of innovation, the immortal rule of effortlessness keeps on directing the formation of points of interaction that reverberate with and take special care of the different necessities of clients all over the planet.

4.3 User experience and the platform's intuitive design

Client experience (UX) and natural plan are focal support points in the making of computerized stages that reverberate with clients, cultivating commitment and fulfillment. In this investigation, we dive into the unpredictable connection between client experience and natural plan, analyzing how the consistent reconciliation of these standards shapes the manner in which clients associate with different advanced interfaces. From sites and portable applications to programming stages and then some, the union of UX and natural plan assumes a vital part in characterizing the achievement and reception of computerized items.

At its quintessence, client experience incorporates the sum of a client's collaboration with an item or administration, including each touchpoint and part of commitment. It reaches out past the visual style to envelop the close to home and down to earth parts of the client's excursion. Client experience configuration looks to make significant and positive associations, taking into account the client's necessities, objectives, and assumptions all through their commitment with the stage.

Instinctive plan, then again, alludes to the production of points of interaction that are intrinsically straightforward and explore. An instinctive plan expects client conduct, lining up with normal human senses and mental models. It limits the expectation to learn and adapt, permitting clients to easily collaborate with the stage. The coordination of natural plan standards inside the more extensive system of client experience establishes a climate where clients feel good as well as enabled in their connections.

The visual part of a computerized stage is the primary resource for clients, and it establishes the vibe for their general insight. A very much created visual plan adds to the stylish allure of the connection point, making a positive underlying feeling.

The variety range, typography, and generally speaking format assume pivotal parts in laying out the visual personality of the stage. Consistency in visual components across various segments of the connection point adds to a strong and brought together plan, upgrading the general client experience.

The client's excursion through a computerized stage is much of the time nonlinear, enveloping different errands, activities, and choice focuses. The route plan of the stage is a critical determinant of how easily clients can move starting with one segment then onto the next. Instinctive route includes a reasonable and intelligent construction, where clients can undoubtedly find data or highlights without getting lost. The arrangement of menus, buttons, and intuitive components ought to line up with client assumptions, limiting the requirement for broad investigation.

Consider the route plan of a site, where the menu design, connections, and source of inspiration buttons guide clients through various pages. A natural route framework guarantees that clients can easily find what they are searching for, whether it's data, items, or administrations. Compelling route is especially critical in online business stages, where consistent development between item classes, shopping baskets, and checkout processes adds to a positive client experience.

The standard of effortlessness, as examined prior, assumes an imperative part in both client experience and natural plan. A jumbled and excessively complex point of interaction can overpower clients, prompting dissatisfaction and separation. Straightforwardness includes refining the plan to its fundamental parts, introducing data in a reasonable and compact way. From a client experience point of view, effortlessness decreases mental burden, making it more straightforward for clients to fathom and explore the point of interaction.

Additionally, straightforwardness in plan is intently attached to the idea of findability - the simplicity with which clients can find data or elements inside the stage. Instinctive plan guarantees that clients can find what they need without superfluous exertion. The association of content, the utilization of distinct names, and the situation of search functionalities add to the findability of data, improving the general client experience.

The idea of affordance, presented by analyst James J. Gibson, is basic to instinctive plan. Affordances are the apparent or genuine properties of an article that propose how it very well may be utilized. With regards to computerized interfaces, affordances guide clients in figuring out the usefulness of various components. For instance, an interactive button ought to outwardly convey its interactiveness, showing to clients that it very well may be interfaced with. The unmistakable show of affordances adds to the instinctive idea of the plan, lining up with client assumptions and ways of behaving.

Criticism components are indispensable to client experience and natural plan. It would be ideal for clients to get clear and opportune criticism on their activities inside the stage. Viewable signs, for example, changes in button appearance upon drift, stacking markers, or achievement messages, illuminate clients that their cooperations have been perceived and are creating the planned results. Compelling criticism adds to a feeling of responsiveness, lessening vulnerability and improving the general client experience.

With regards to web structures and information input, giving continuous criticism on the legitimacy of client input is a sign of instinctive plan. On the off chance that a client enters a wrong email configuration or skirts an expected field, quick criticism assists them with redressing mistakes without presenting the structure and hang tight for a reaction. This iterative criticism circle diminishes erosion in client cooperations and adds to a smoother in general insight.

The idea of client streams is integral to both client experience and natural plan. A client stream maps the series of stages a client takes to achieve a particular errand inside the stage. Whether it's finishing a buy, pursuing a pamphlet, or getting to explicit substance, a very much planned client stream considers the consistent grouping of moves that clients are probably going to make. Instinctive client streams diminish erosion, permitting clients to advance through undertakings with insignificant exertion and mental burden.

Consider the client stream of a versatile banking application. The plan ought to instinctively direct clients through the method involved with financial records adjusts, moving assets, or taking care of bills. The position of buttons, the lucidity of names, and the grouping of steps ought to line up with clients' assumptions, lessening the requirement for unreasonable investigation or help. A compelling client stream adds to a positive client experience and supports the instinct of the plan.

Consistency is a key rule that supports both client experience and instinctive plan. Consistency includes keeping a uniform show of components and ways of behaving across various segments of the stage. At the point when clients experience reliable plan designs, they can construct mental models that apply to different pieces of the connection point. This consistency improves the client experience, as clients can certainly explore various segments without experiencing surprising varieties.

Consistency applies to both visual components and intuitive ways of behaving. For instance, the arrangement of route menus, the utilization of variety plans, and the way of behaving of intuitive components like buttons ought to stay reliable all through the stage. Steady plan adds to a feeling of intelligence, diminishing the mental burden related with learning new examples or adjusting to changes inside the point of interaction.

With regards to portable applications, the adherence to stage explicit plan rules adds to both consistency and instinctive plan. Clients familiar with the plan examples of a specific working framework (iOS or Android) expect applications to line up with the shows of that framework. Observing stage explicit rules guarantees that clients can use their current information and propensities, encouraging a natural encounter.

Personalization is a developing aspect in client experience and natural plan. Personalization includes fitting the point of interaction to match the inclinations, ways of behaving, and needs of individual clients. By utilizing information on client communications, inclinations, and socioeconomics, stages can convey redid encounters that reverberate with clients on a more private level. Personalization improves client commitment and fulfillment, adding to a positive generally speaking experience.

Consider the personalization elements of streaming stages like Netflix or music administrations like Spotify. These stages dissect client conduct, like watched shows, enjoyed tunes, or perusing history, to suggest customized content. The natural plan of these stages reaches out to how proposals are introduced, guaranteeing that clients feel a feeling of commonality and pertinence in their customized content feeds.

Openness is a vital part of both client experience and natural plan. An available plan guarantees that people with incapacities can draw in with the stage successfully. From a client experience point of view, openness includes establishing a comprehensive climate where all clients, no matter what their capacities, can explore, collaborate, and get esteem from the stage.

Instinctive plan lines up with openness by making points of interaction detectable, operable, reasonable, and powerful for clients with assorted capacities. Contemplations, for example, giving elective text to pictures, guaranteeing console route, and offering high differentiation choices add to a natural and available plan. By focusing on openness, stages exhibit a pledge to inclusivity, growing their scope to a more extensive and more different client base.

The job of microinteractions in client experience and natural plan ought not be disregarded. Microinteractions are unpretentious, single-use activitys or criticism systems that happen in light of explicit client activities. While apparently little, these microinteractions add to the general client experience by giving visual and material.

Chapter 5

Security and Privacy

In the quickly advancing scene of the 21st 100 years, the entwined ideas of safety and protection have become principal concerns. As innovation propels at an exceptional speed, people and associations end up exploring an unpredictable trap of difficulties to defend delicate data and safeguard individual limits. The computerized age, set apart by interconnected gadgets and universal web-based presence, has introduced another period where the fragile harmony among security and protection is continually under a magnifying glass.

In the domain of online protection, the stakes have never been higher. The digitization of pretty much every part of our lives, from monetary exchanges to medical care records, has made a tremendous scene of information powerless to double-dealing. As digital dangers become more complex and unavoidable, the requirement for hearty safety efforts has turned into a major problem. The conventional ideal models of safety, when revolved around actual obstructions and unmistakable resources, have extended to envelop virtual domains where immaterial information holds tremendous worth.

One of the crucial difficulties in the domain of safety is the never-ending wait-and-see game among trend-setters and noxious entertainers. As innovation advances, so do the abilities of those looking to take advantage of weaknesses. From state-supported digital assaults to monetarily inspired hacking, the inspirations driving breaks are different, making the protection against them a perplexing and complex undertaking. The idea of a "zero-trust" model has acquired unmistakable quality, underlining the need to check anybody attempting to get to frameworks and information, no matter what their area or organization.

In this advanced age, where information is many times considered the new money, the assurance of individual data has become inseparable from defending individual protection. The rising predominance of web-based entertainment, internet business, and online administrations has prompted a tremendous gathering of individual information by enterprises and legislatures the same. This has started banters about the moral utilization of such data and the degree to which people ought to have command over their advanced characters.

Legislatures all over the planet are wrestling with the test of creating regulation that finds some kind of harmony between guaranteeing public safety and maintaining the protection privileges of their residents. The pressure between observation measures pointed toward forestalling crimes and the right to protection has led to banters about the constraints of state intercession. The approach of advances like facial acknowledgment and mass reconnaissance frameworks has additionally filled these conversations, as they raise worries about the disintegration of individual namelessness openly spaces.

The worldwide idea of the web adds an extra layer of intricacy to the protection scene. Information, when kept to public lines, presently streams flawlessly across the globe. This interconnectedness requires global participation and arrangements to address the difficulties of cross-line information streams and the extraterritorial reach of guidelines. The European Association's Overall Information Security Guideline (GDPR) stands apart as a milestone work to blend information insurance regulations across part states and has impacted comparative drives around the world.

As the computerized biological system turns out to be progressively many-sided, people end up exploring a sensitive harmony between the comfort of innovation and the protection of their security. The multiplication of savvy gadgets, from indoor regulators to wearable wellness trackers, brings up issues about the degree to which people will exchange individual information for the advantages of improved network and customized administrations. The idea of "reconnaissance private enterprise," begat by researcher Shoshana Zuboff, depicts a peculiarity where client information is commodified for monetary addition, testing conventional thoughts of protection in the computerized time.

The business world, as well, isn't resistant to the difficulties presented by the advancing scene of safety and protection. Undertakings should wrestle with the double liability of safeguarding their touchy data and regarding the protection assumptions for their clients and workers. Information breaks risk monetary security as well as dissolve trust, a significant component in any business relationship. As guidelines fix and shoppers become seriously knowing about the treatment of their information, organizations face a developing basic to focus on network safety and protection as indispensable parts of their corporate technique.

The coming of man-made consciousness (artificial intelligence) and AI presents the two open doors and dangers in the domain of safety and security. While these advances hold the commitment of upgrading danger discovery and reaction capacities, they additionally raise worries about the potential for predisposition and segregation in robotized dynamic cycles. The straightforwardness of simulated intelligence calculations and the moral contemplations encompassing their utilization become basic variables in moderating these dangers and cultivating public trust.

With regards to public safety, the crossing point of innovation and international affairs presents novel difficulties. Online protection dangers, when restricted to virtual areas, presently can possibly influence basic foundation, financial security, and, surprisingly, international relations. State-supported digital assaults have become instruments of political influence, provoking countries to foster hostile and guarded digital capacities. The reconciliation of digital fighting procedures into customary military teachings highlights the developing idea of safety challenges in the 21st hundred years.

The shift towards remote work, advanced by worldwide occasions like the Coronavirus pandemic, has additionally elevated the significance of online protection. As associations embrace adaptable work plans, the assault surface grows, making new weaknesses for malignant entertainers to take advantage of. Getting remote access, safeguarding delicate information on the way, and guaranteeing the flexibility of virtual joint effort stages have become central focuses for network safety experts entrusted with adjusting to the advancing idea of the cutting edge work environment.

In the journey for improved security, the job of encryption arises as a foundation of computerized safeguard. Start to finish encryption, specifically, is proclaimed as a strong component for shielding correspondence from unapproved access, whether by malignant programmers or state reconnaissance. Be that as it may, the discussion over encryption additionally envelops worries about its possible abuse by crooks to disguise unlawful exercises, provoking conversations about the sensitive harmony among protection and public wellbeing.

As the limits among physical and computerized domains obscure, the idea of "shrewd urban communities" arises as a proving ground for coordinated security and protection arrangements. The sending of sensors, IoT gadgets, and information examination in metropolitan conditions guarantees further developed effectiveness, maintainability, and personal satisfaction. Be that as it may, this vision accompanies intrinsic difficulties connected with information administration, assent, and the potential for mass reconnaissance. Finding some kind of harmony that use innovation for cultural advantage while regarding individual protection turns into a urgent thought for the planners of brilliant city drives.

The training and consciousness of people assume a critical part in the general security and protection scene. Digital cleanliness rehearses, for example, solid secret word the executives, customary programming updates, and familiarity with phishing strategies, contribute altogether to individual flexibility against digital dangers. Furthermore, drives to instruct clients about their computerized privileges and the ramifications of sharing individual data cultivate a more educated and engaged society.

All in all, the entwined elements of safety and protection in the 21st century present a diverse test that ranges mechanical, moral, lawful, and cultural aspects. As the advanced scene keeps on developing, so should our ways to deal with getting delicate data and protecting individual security. The cooperative endeavors of states, organizations, technologists, and people are fundamental to explore the intricacies of this computerized age and produce a way that maintains the standards of safety and protection as one with the fast speed of mechanical advancement.

5.1 Examination of WhatsApp's commitment to user privacy

In the contemporary computerized scene, where correspondence stages assume a crucial part in interfacing people worldwide, the issue of client protection has turned into a focal concern. WhatsApp, a broadly utilized informing application claimed by Meta (previously Facebook), has confronted investigation and commendation the same for its obligation to client security. This assessment dives into the different aspects of WhatsApp's way to deal with client security, dissecting its elements, contentions, and the developing scene of information assurance in the advanced period.

At the core of WhatsApp's protection model is start to finish encryption, a component intended to get clients' messages from being gotten to by anybody other than the planned beneficiary. This implies that even WhatsApp itself can't peruse the items in messages traded between clients. Start to finish encryption is a strong safety effort that guarantees the protection and privacy of discussions, lining up with the developing interest for secure correspondence during a time set apart by digital dangers and information breaks.

WhatsApp's obligation to security is additionally accentuated by its refusal to store clients' messages on its servers. When a message is conveyed, it is erased from the organization's servers, diminishing the gamble of unapproved access. This plan decision recognizes WhatsApp from other informing stages that might hold client information for different purposes, like further developing administrations or designated publicizing.

Notwithstanding message encryption, WhatsApp has presented elements like vanishing messages, giving clients the choice to set a clock for messages to erase after an assigned period consequently. While this element improves client command over their information, it likewise brings up issues about the lastingness of advanced correspondence and the potential for messages to be utilized in accidental ways.

Nonetheless, WhatsApp's protection rehearses have not been without contention. One striking occurrence was the presentation of a security strategy update in January 2021, which prompted broad worries and reaction from clients. The update incited clients to consent to impart specific information to Meta, including data connected with exchanges and communications with organizations on the stage. The apparent change in information sharing practices started a worldwide clamor and a flood in clients investigating elective informing applications.

WhatsApp answered the reaction by explaining that the update didn't influence the security of clients' very own discussions and that start to finish encryption stayed in salvageable shape. The organization credited the progressions to work with more consistent correspondence with organizations on the stage, underscoring that individual messages and calls wouldn't be open to Meta.

Notwithstanding these affirmations, the episode highlighted the sensitive equilibrium organizations should strike between financial matters, client experience, and protection assumptions.

The protection strategy contention likewise pointed out the job of informed assent in the advanced domain. Clients, frequently immersed with extensive terms of administration arrangements and security strategies, may not completely handle the ramifications of information sharing practices. This occurrence provoked conversations about the requirement for more clear correspondence and straightforwardness in illuminating clients about how their information is gathered, utilized, and shared.

Because of the protection strategy commotion, a few clients moved to elective informing stages that situated themselves as security centered other options. This shift featured the meaning of client trust and the effect of protection worries on the serious scene of informing applications. Organizations offering secure and confidential correspondence administrations tracked down a chance to benefit from the discontent of clients looking for choices that adjusted all the more intimately with their protection inclinations.

Past individual client concerns, WhatsApp's obligation to security is likewise assessed inside the more extensive setting of administrative systems. The Overall Information Assurance Guideline (GDPR), executed by the European Association, sets rigid principles for the security of individual information and the privileges of people. As a worldwide stage, WhatsApp should explore an interwoven of global guidelines that fluctuate in their way to deal with information security.

WhatsApp's parent organization, Meta, has confronted lawful difficulties and fines connected with security issues. In 2019, the U.S. Government Exchange Commission (FTC) forced a $5 billion punishment on Facebook (preceding its rebranding as Meta) for security infringement, including the misusing of client information. This episode featured the administrative investigation looked by significant tech organizations and the likely monetary results of protection breaks.

The crossing point of protection and publicizing likewise assumes a part in assessing WhatsApp's obligation to client security. While WhatsApp itself doesn't show advertisements in private talks, its combination with the more extensive Meta environment brings up issues about the expected utilization of WhatsApp information for designated promoting on other Meta stages. The organization has accentuated the partition among WhatsApp and Meta's publicizing business, expressing that client information from WhatsApp isn't utilized to illuminate promotion focusing on different stages.

Notwithstanding, the interconnected idea of Meta's administrations raises worries about the conglomeration of client information across stages, possibly making a far reaching profile of people's web-based conduct. As the limits between various administrations obscure, the difficulties of guaranteeing security become more intricate, expecting organizations to carry out hearty shields to safeguard client data.

WhatsApp's obligation to client security is likewise examined with regards to policing and government reconnaissance. The stage has distributed straightforwardness reports itemizing the quantity of solicitations got from states for client information and the moves made accordingly. Adjusting the need to help out real policing while at the same time protecting client security is a sensitive undertaking that informing stages, including WhatsApp, should explore.

The advancing scene of protection and security in the computerized age presents new contemplations, for example, the effect of arising advancements like man-made consciousness and AI. As these advances become essential to the improvement of correspondence stages, questions emerge about the moral utilization of man-made intelligence in directing substance, distinguishing misuse, and guaranteeing a safe web-based climate without compromising client protection.

Looking forward, the direction of WhatsApp's obligation to client security is probably going to be formed by a powerful interchange of innovative progressions, administrative turns of events, and developing client assumptions. The stage's reaction to arising difficulties, its flexibility to changing protection standards, and its capacity to remake and keep up with client trust in the result of contentions will be key elements impacting its remaining in the cutthroat scene of informing applications.

All in all, the assessment of WhatsApp's obligation to client security uncovers a perplexing exchange of elements, debates, and the more extensive scene of computerized correspondence. While the stage has executed powerful safety efforts, for example, start to finish encryption and client information minimization, it has likewise confronted difficulties connected with protection strategy refreshes and the more extensive ramifications of its mix with the Meta environment. As clients and controllers request more prominent straightforwardness and command over private information, the eventual fate of WhatsApp's security practices will probably be formed by a persistent discourse between mechanical development, administrative structures, and the developing assumptions for a protection cognizant client base.

5.2 Implementation of end-to-end encryption

The execution of start to finish encryption (E2EE) addresses a crucial headway in the domain of computerized correspondence and protection. This vigorous safety effort has become inseparable from safeguarding touchy data from unapproved access, guaranteeing that main the planned beneficiaries can translate the encoded information.

As the advanced scene develops and the requirement for secure correspondence increases, the assessment of the execution of start to finish encryption becomes basic, including its mechanical underpinnings, suggestions for client protection, and the more extensive cultural and administrative setting.

At its center, start to finish encryption is a cryptographic procedure that gets correspondence by scrambling the substance at the shipper's gadget and decoding it just at the beneficiary's gadget. This implies that the middle person administration working with the correspondence, whether it be an informing application or an email supplier, can't get to the plaintext information. The encryption keys, which are expected to interpret the data, are just held by the imparting parties, adding an additional layer of safety to the transmission of messages.

The execution of start to finish encryption depends on complex numerical calculations to encode the data in a manner that is computationally infeasible to switch without the comparing unscrambling key. This guarantees that regardless of whether the scrambled information is captured during transmission, it stays unintelligible to any unapproved substances. Outstanding cryptographic conventions, like the Sign Convention, have acquired far and wide reception for carrying out start to finish encryption in different informing applications.

One of the critical benefits of start to finish encryption is its capacity to alleviate the dangers related with interference and snoopping. In customary correspondence models, where messages cross through servers and organizations, there exists a possible weakness for malignant entertainers or even specialist co-ops to get to the substance of the correspondence. Start to finish encryption takes out this gamble by delivering the captured information incoherent without the decoding key, giving a huge lift to the classification of computerized correspondence.

Informing applications that focus on client security frequently influence start to finish encryption as a focal element. WhatsApp, Sign, and Message are conspicuous instances of stages that have embraced this innovation to furnish clients with a solid and confidential method for correspondence. WhatsApp, specifically, plays had a urgent impact in promoting start to finish encryption by executing it as the default setting for all messages traded on the stage.

The far reaching reception of start to finish encryption has, in any case, experienced difficulties and discussions. Policing and legislatures have communicated worries that such solid encryption can hinder their capacity to explore and forestall crimes. The pressure between protection advocates, who champion the option to get correspondence, and policing looking for instruments for powerful wrongdoing counteraction highlights the complex moral and lawful contemplations encompassing the execution of start to finish encryption.

With regards to client security, the execution of start to finish encryption tends to longstanding worries about unapproved observation and information breaks. The disclosures of mass reconnaissance programs by government organizations, as exemplified by Edward Snowden's divulgences, set off an uplifted familiarity with the requirement for strong protection shields. Start to finish encryption arose as a mechanical reaction to the disintegration of trust brought about by these disclosures, enabling people to impart unafraid of unjustifiable observation.

While start to finish encryption fundamentally upgrades the security of computerized correspondence, it isn't without its difficulties. The safe transmission of messages is dependent upon the assurance of encryption keys. On the off chance that a gadget is compromised, either through malware or actual access, the privacy of the correspondence can be compromised. This weakness features the significance of getting the gadgets that partake in start to finish encoded correspondence and carrying out extra safety efforts, like gadget confirmation and secure key stockpiling.

In addition, the client experience of start to finish encoded correspondence has suggestions for its far and wide reception. While protection cognizant clients value the improved security, others might find the extra advances, for example, key confirmation processes, awkward. Finding some kind of harmony between powerful safety efforts and easy to use points of interaction is difficult for designers looking to make start to finish encryption open to a more extensive crowd.

The execution of start to finish encryption isn't restricted to message based correspondence. Voice and video calls, too as record moves, can likewise profit from the additional layer of safety given by E2EE. The expansion of this innovation to mixed media content guarantees that an exhaustive scope of computerized cooperations stays secret and secure. As the advanced scene turns out to be progressively visual and sight and sound driven, the job of start to finish encryption in defending different types of correspondence turns out to be much more basic.

The arrangement of start to finish encryption in different correspondence stages lines up with advancing cultural assumptions about protection. Clients are turning out to be more aware of the information they create and share internet, provoking an interest for administrations that focus on protection and security. The outcome of informing applications like Sign, which acquired broad prominence because of its obligation to start to finish encryption and information minimization, represents the developing business sector for security driven specialized apparatuses.

The execution of start to finish encryption likewise meets with the more extensive talk on information possession and control. In a scene where client information has turned into an important ware, people are progressively looking for stages that enable them to hold command over their computerized impression.

Start to finish encryption, by configuration, lines up with this longing for control, as it guarantees that the substance of correspondence stays inside the circle of the conveying parties, decreasing the dependence on outsider specialist co-ops to protect delicate data.

In any case, the idealistic vision of start to finish encryption as an impenetrable safeguard shielding computerized correspondence faces difficulties from different quarters. State run administrations and administrative bodies, worried about the likely abuse of secure correspondence channels for criminal operations, have investigated ways of offsetting protection privileges with the basic for public safety. The strain between these goals frequently appears in banters about the presentation of secondary passages or uncommon access components that would permit approved elements to sidestep encryption under unambiguous conditions.

The proposition for secondary passages, or underlying weaknesses to work with access, has been met areas of strength for with from security advocates and the network safety local area. The contention against indirect accesses rotates around the inborn dangers they present. Bringing deliberate weaknesses into encryption frameworks, even determined to give access just to approved elements, makes a road for abuse by pernicious entertainers. The split the difference of such indirect accesses might actually prompt far and wide information breaks and subvert the very safety efforts they intend to protect.

The legitimate scene encompassing the execution of start to finish encryption is set apart by an interwoven of guidelines and contrasting methodologies across locales. A few nations have sanctioned regulation that expressly supports or commands the utilization of start to finish encryption for specific kinds of correspondence. Others have tried to control or limit its utilization, refering to worries about the expected impediment of policing.

In the European Association, the Overall Information Assurance Guideline (GDPR) underlines the significance of information security and the freedoms of people to get and confidential correspondence. The GDPR's rigid prerequisites for the legitimate handling of individual information have impacted the security practices of organizations working inside the EU and then some. The worldwide idea of computerized correspondence and the interconnectedness of online administrations imply that organizations frequently explore a perplexing scene of administrative consistence.

The execution of start to finish encryption additionally brings up issues about the responsibility of specialist organizations. In situations where stages offer scrambled correspondence benefits, the obligation regarding client information movements to the actual clients. While this lines up with the guideline of engaging people to control their information, it likewise requires a degree of computerized proficiency and obligation that not all clients might have. Guaranteeing that clients know about the ramifications of start to finish encryption, including the significance of safely overseeing encryption keys, turns into a pivotal part of security instruction.

The appearance of quantum processing acquaints another aspect with the talk on the security of encryption calculations. While current cryptographic norms depend on the computational intricacy of specific numerical issues, quantum PCs can possibly tackle these issues dramatically quicker than old style PCs. This raises worries about the drawn out security of existing encryption conventions and the requirement for the advancement of quantum-safe cryptographic calculations.

All in all, the execution of start to finish encryption addresses a foundation in the continuous development of computerized correspondence and security. This cryptographic method, intended to tie down correspondence from one finish to another, has turned into a characterizing component of protection centered informing applications and communication.

5.3 Impact on user trust and global adoption

The effect of start to finish encryption (E2EE) on client trust and worldwide reception is a diverse part of its general impact on computerized correspondence. As people and associations explore an undeniably interconnected and information driven world, the affirmation of secure and confidential correspondence has become principal. Analyzing how the execution of start to finish encryption resounds with client trust and its suggestions for worldwide reception reveals insight into the more extensive cultural, social, and mechanical elements molding the computerized scene.

Client trust is primary to the progress of any correspondence stage, and the reconciliation of start to finish encryption assumes a crucial part in cultivating and keeping up with that trust. The confirmation that individual and delicate data stays classified and out of reach to unapproved substances ingrains a feeling of safety among clients. Stages that focus on security through the sending of E2EE are bound to gather the trust of a client base progressively mindful of the ramifications of information breaks and protection encroachments.

The developing accentuation on client protection, driven by high-profile information breaks, disclosures of mass observation, and advancing security guidelines, has elevated the interest for secure specialized instruments. Start to finish encryption, with its commitment of secret and alter safe correspondence, lines up with the moving assumptions for clients who look for command over their own information. The execution of this innovation turns into an unmistakable exhibition of a stage's obligation to client driven security rehearses.

Informing applications that have advocated start to finish encryption, like WhatsApp and Signal, have seen expanded client reception and maintenance. The broad utilization of these stages for individual and expert correspondence highlights the reverberation of start to finish encryption with clients who focus on protection in their computerized connections. The fuse of E2EE as a default setting in such applications mirrors an essential choice to make security the standard, molding client assumptions and setting a benchmark for the business.

The effect of start to finish encryption on client trust reaches out past individual inclinations to envelop the reputational remaining of the specialist co-op. Organizations that focus on client protection and put resources into vigorous safety efforts, including E2EE, improve their validity and separate themselves in a cutthroat market. Trust, once disintegrated by security concerns or information breaks, is trying to revamp, making the execution of innovations like start to finish encryption an essential basic for stages looking for supported achievement.

In the domain of worldwide reception, the job of start to finish encryption turns out to be significantly more articulated as stages take special care of different social, legitimate, and administrative settings. Various locales have particular perspectives toward security, and how much start to finish encryption lines up with social assumptions fundamentally impacts its reception on a worldwide scale. In locales where protection is exceptionally esteemed, the execution of E2EE is probably going to be met with energy, adding to the stage's acknowledgment and utilization.

In any case, the worldwide scene likewise presents difficulties, as shifting administrative structures and government perspectives toward encryption make a mind boggling embroidery of legitimate contemplations. A few nations might areas of strength for see as a prevention to policing public safety endeavors, prompting discussions and likely limitations on the utilization of start to finish encryption. Finding some kind of harmony between client protection, genuine policing, and consistence with neighborhood guidelines turns into a fragile errand for stages working on a worldwide scale.

The effect of start to finish encryption on worldwide reception is complicatedly attached to the apparent compromises between security, protection, and convenience. While protection cognizant clients might focus on stages that focus on start to finish encryption, others might gauge the accommodation of purpose and extra highlights against the apparent advantages of improved security. Finding some kind of harmony is a critical thought for informing applications looking for boundless acknowledgment in different client socioeconomics.

The reception of start to finish encryption isn't bound to individual correspondence however reaches out to expert and business use cases. In a time where remote work and computerized coordinated effort have become omnipresent, the safe trade of delicate data is a basic prerequisite. Stages that coordinate start to finish encryption in their specialized devices furnish associations with a safe climate for conversations, record sharing, and joint effort, imparting trust in the security of exclusive and private data.

The effect of start to finish encryption on client trust is additionally interlaced with the developing idea of digital dangers. As cyberattacks become more refined and information penetrates progressively normal, clients are turning out to be really knowing about the safety efforts executed by the stages they draw in with.

The commitment of start to finish encryption fills in as a substantial consolation against the possible outcomes of unapproved access and information double-dealing, impacting client impression of a stage's obligation to their security.

While the advantages of start to finish encryption are clear, its execution doesn't come without difficulties and contemplations. The possible abuse of secure correspondence channels for unlawful exercises brings up moral and legitimate issues. Finding some kind of harmony between the protection freedoms of clients and the requirement for cultural wellbeing and security turns into a nuanced conversation that includes partners going from protection promoters and innovation organizations to policing and policymakers.

The effect of start to finish encryption on client trust is likewise dependent upon the advancing idea of innovation and the rise of new dangers. As encryption calculations mature and quantum registering presents expected difficulties to current cryptographic norms, the versatility and responsibility of stages to remain in front of arising chances become significant. Clients' trust is contingent on current safety efforts as well as on the stage's capacity to actually develop and address future dangers.

With regards to social informing, the effect of start to finish encryption reaches out to the insurance of client produced content, including message, pictures, recordings, and voice messages. The confirmation that such happy remaining parts private and unavailable to outsiders adds to a feeling of pride and control among clients. Stages that focus on the security of media content through start to finish encryption build up the thought that clients reserve the option to convey uninhibitedly without the apprehension about ridiculous observation or information double-dealing.

The effect of start to finish encryption on client trust is additionally highlighted by the straightforwardness and correspondence endeavors of specialist co-ops. Stages that transparently convey their protection rehearses, go through free security reviews, and draw in with their client networks to address concerns show a pledge to straight-forwardness. Client trust isn't exclusively based on the presence of safety highlights like start to finish encryption yet additionally on the stage's capacity to impart these elements really and construct a story of dependability.

The powerful exchange between start to finish encryption and client trust is reflected in the occasional discussions and discussions encompassing security rehearses. Episodes, for example, the WhatsApp security strategy update in 2021, which prompted boundless worries and client movement to elective stages, highlight the effect of protection related choices on client trust. The correspondence of security strategy changes, the lucidity of terms of administration, and the responsiveness of stages to client input become necessary parts of molding and keeping up with client trust.

The effect of start to finish encryption on client trust isn't restricted to individual clients however stretches out to institutional and undertaking clients. Organizations, especially those managing delicate data and licensed innovation, put an exceptional on specialized devices that give a solid climate. The confirmation that start to finish encryption safeguards private conversations, client data, and exclusive information adds to the reception of such stages in proficient settings.

Looking forward, the effect of start to finish encryption on client trust will keep on developing in light of mechanical headways, administrative turns of events, and changing client assumptions. The continuous discourse between security advocates, innovation organizations, policymakers, and clients will shape the direction of advanced correspondence and the job of encryption in defending client trust. As the computerized scene develops, the combination of start to finish encryption will probably turn into an inexorably indispensable part of client assumptions and a vital differentiator for correspondence stages trying to fabricate and keep a dedicated client base.

Chapter 6

Cultural Adaptability

Social flexibility in the domain of innovation and correspondence has arisen as a basic thought in a time set apart by worldwide interconnectedness. As advanced stages and administrations penetrate different social scenes, the capacity to adjust and reverberate with the qualities, standards, and inclinations of various social orders becomes instrumental in making far reaching acknowledgment and progress. Looking at the idea of social flexibility dives into the manners by which innovation organizations, correspondence stages, and computerized administrations explore the intricacies of assorted societies, tending to difficulties and cultivating inclusivity.

Social versatility envelops the limit of innovation and correspondence stages to take care of the particular requirements and assumptions for clients from different social foundations. It goes past simple interpretation of content into various dialects and stretches out to a more profound comprehension of social subtleties, social practices, and responsive qualities. In an interconnected world, where computerized administrations are gotten to by people from different districts, the capacity to adjust to social variety turns into an essential basic for organizations looking for worldwide importance.

Language, as an essential part of culture, assumes a focal part in social versatility. Past giving multilingual points of interaction, socially versatile stages perceive the significance of setting, colloquial articulations, and semantic subtleties that might shift across societies. Precise and socially touchy interpretation is fundamental for UIs as well as for content, interchanges, and backing materials. Organizations putting resources into powerful limitation endeavors show a promise to separating language hindrances and drawing in with clients in a way that reverberates with their social setting.

UI configuration is one more significant element of social flexibility. Various societies might have unmistakable inclinations with respect to variety plans, images, and format structures. Adjusting the plan to line up with social style improves the client experience and keeps away from accidental social harshness. For instance, varieties might convey explicit social implications, and a connection point that regards these social affiliations is bound to be generally welcomed by clients from that culture.

The joining of socially significant substance is a critical part of social flexibility. This stretches out to the accessibility of content that mirrors the social variety of clients, including pictures, delineations, and media components.

Stages that curate happy with aversion to social standards and variety enhance the client experience as well as add to a feeling of inclusivity. This inclusivity cultivates a positive view of the stage as one that qualities and regards the social personalities of its clients.

The flexibility of innovation to assorted social settings isn't restricted to style and language yet in addition reaches out to usefulness. Social contrasts might impact client inclinations concerning highlights, functionalities, and the general client venture. Stages that focus on social flexibility effectively look for client criticism from various areas and integrate this contribution to the iterative plan and improvement processes. This client driven approach guarantees that the stage lines up with the assumptions and use examples of assorted social networks.

Accepted practices and correspondence styles shift fundamentally across societies. Stages that perceive and oblige these varieties in correspondence styles are better situated to work with significant communications. For example, a few societies might esteem immediate and unequivocal correspondence, while others might favor more backhanded or implied types of articulation. Understanding these subtleties is vital in planning specialized apparatuses that take care of the assorted manners by which people from various societies draw in with each other.

The crossing point of innovation and culture turns out to be especially articulated in the domain of online entertainment. Social stages, by their tendency, are spaces where people express their social characters, share social substance, and take part in diverse connections. Socially versatile virtual entertainment stages oblige different types of articulation as well as effectively advance social trade and understanding. The capacity to explore social awarenesses, moderate substance dependably, and cultivate positive multifaceted cooperations characterizes the progress of social stages in assorted worldwide settings.

The social flexibility of innovation is likewise apparent in the domain of web based business. Online business stages that take care of assorted social inclinations, installment techniques, and shopping propensities are bound to prevail in worldwide business sectors. This flexibility stretches out to contemplations like the introduction of items, estimating shows, and socially fitting promoting systems. By lining up with the social assumptions for their client base, internet business stages improve client trust and improve the probability of effective exchanges.

Social flexibility turns out to be especially critical with regards to arising innovations like man-made consciousness (computer based intelligence) and augmented reality (VR). Man-made intelligence calculations that power proposal frameworks, content curation, and customized encounters should be prepared on different datasets that include an expansive range of social settings. Predisposition in artificial intelligence calculations, whether unexpected or fundamental, can prompt imbalances and build up social generalizations. Socially versatile simulated intelligence requires progressing examination, moral contemplations, and a pledge to variety in information assortment and algorithmic direction.

Computer generated reality, with its vivid nature, offers potential open doors for social encounters and communications. Socially versatile VR applications can ship clients to virtual conditions that reflect assorted social settings, verifiable settings, and imaginative articulations. This can possibly encourage culturally diverse comprehension and sympathy. In any case, it likewise raises moral contemplations connected with the appointment of social images, the potential for generalizing, and the requirement for deferential portrayal in virtual spaces.

In the instructive space, innovation has turned into an incredible asset for learning and information spread. Socially versatile instructive innovation perceives the significance of socially important substance, various points of view, and comprehensive academic methodologies. This reaches out to the plan of instructive materials, the fuse of socially assorted models, and the thought of various learning styles pervasive in different social settings.

One of the difficulties in accomplishing social versatility lies in the requirement for a nuanced comprehension of societies, which are dynamic, complex, and continually developing. Generalizations and speculations can prompt misinterpretations and coincidentally sustain social inclinations. Organizations focused on social flexibility put resources into social skill preparing for their groups, participate in multifaceted examination, and look for associations with nearby specialists to guarantee an educated and conscious way to deal with social variety.

Exploring legitimate and administrative scenes is a basic piece of social flexibility, particularly for worldwide innovation organizations. Various areas might have fluctuating legitimate systems connected with information insurance, security, content balance, and client freedoms. Adjusting innovation stages to conform to these guidelines while regarding social standards and assumptions requires an extensive comprehension of the lawful complexities of each social setting.

The effect of social flexibility is apparent in the examples of overcoming adversity of innovation organizations that have successfully fitted their contributions to assorted social business sectors. For instance, web-based entertainment stages like WeChat in China and Line in Japan have accomplished predominance by coordinating social inclinations, neighborhood dialects, and district explicit highlights. These stages give natural client encounters as well as consolidate components that reverberate with the social characters of their client base.

Social versatility likewise crosses with corporate social obligation (CSR) and moral contemplations. Organizations that focus on social versatility as a component of their business methodology are bound to take part in socially mindful practices that line up with the qualities and assumptions for the networks they serve. This incorporates drives connected with variety and consideration, local area commitment, and charity that decidedly influence the social texture of social orders.

The effect of social versatility stretches out past the innovation business to envelop different areas, including medical care, money, and administration. In medical care, for instance, innovation arrangements that are socially versatile can connect holes in medical care access, work on quiet correspondence, and improve the adequacy of well-being mediations by lining up with social standards and practices. Additionally, in the monetary area, innovation stages that oblige assorted monetary propensities, installment inclinations, and social perspectives toward cash are bound to build up some decent momentum in worldwide business sectors.

In the administration and community tech space, social versatility assumes a urgent part in guaranteeing that innovation arrangements work with resident commitment, straightforwardness, and inclusivity. Stages intended to improve city support need to consider the assorted manners by which people from various social foundations draw in with municipal cycles. Socially versatile community tech adds to the democratization of data, urban strengthening, and the fortifying of popularity based foundations.

6.1 WhatsApp's success in different linguistic and cultural contexts

WhatsApp's progress in various semantic and social settings is a demonstration of the stage's versatility and reverberation across different worldwide scenes. As a broadly utilized informing application, WhatsApp has risen above semantic obstructions, social contrasts, and geological limits to turn into a pervasive specialized instrument. Looking at the variables that add to WhatsApp's progress in different etymological and social settings divulges bits of knowledge into the stage's plan, highlights, and key methodologies that have empowered it to flourish in a large number of social conditions.

Language, being a principal part of culture, assumes a significant part in Whats-App's worldwide achievement. WhatsApp's obligation to semantic variety is clear in its multilingual connection point, permitting clients to explore the application in their favored language. The stage upholds a huge swath of dialects, from broadly spoken ones like English, Spanish, and Mandarin to territorial and minority dialects, empowering clients all over the planet to draw in with the application easily in their local tongues.

Also, WhatsApp's help for multilingual correspondence inside discussions upgrades its allure in semantically different areas. The stage consistently obliges the utilization of different dialects inside a solitary talk, mirroring the phonetic elements of numerous multicultural social orders. This component resounds with clients who explore between various dialects in their everyday correspondence, cultivating inclusivity and easy to understand encounters.

WhatsApp's prosperity is additionally credited to its client driven approach in giving elements that adjust social correspondence standards. For example, the stage's presentation of voice informing, a component permitting clients to send recorded voice messages, takes care of social inclinations in districts where spoken correspondence holds critical worth.

This element is especially pertinent in societies with oral customs and where nuanced articulation is preferred passed on through voice rather over text.

The plan straightforwardness of WhatsApp adds to its worldwide achievement, rising above social settings where clients might have differing levels of mechanical commonality. The moderate and natural point of interaction, portrayed by effectively reasonable symbols and a direct talk design, guarantees openness for clients across various age gatherings and innovative proficiencies. This straightforwardness lines up with social assumptions for easy to understand innovation and works with expansive reception.

WhatsApp's prosperity is unpredictably connected to its obligation to client protection and security, esteems that resound all around however might be of specific significance in specific social settings. The stage's execution of start to finish encryption, guaranteeing the classification of client messages, addresses protection concerns common in social orders where people are progressively aware of advanced security. The trust caused by WhatsApp's security highlights adds to its prosperity, particularly in locales where information assurance is a huge thought.

In multicultural conditions, WhatsApp's prosperity is reinforced by its capacity to take care of assorted correspondence styles. Embracing elements like emoticons, stickers, and GIFs, which rise above language hindrances and empower expressive correspondence, reverberates with clients across various societies. These visual components give a widespread language that adds a layer of wealth to computerized discussions, cultivating a feeling of association and understanding.

WhatsApp's outcome in various semantic and social settings is additionally impacted by its versatility to neighborhood correspondence standards. For example, in districts where various leveled connections are stressed, the utilization of notices on WhatsApp fills in as a type of articulation while regarding social orders. Clients can convey their temperament, share updates, or express social subtleties through status messages, giving a limited road to self-articulation inside the stage.

WhatsApp's boundless achievement is intently attached to its thought of social subtleties in highlight advancement. The presentation of highlights like "Last Seen" and read receipts, while questionable in a settings because of protection concerns, lines up with social assumptions in locales where the affirmation of messages and online presence are vital to social elements. These highlights, albeit discretionary, take special care of social standards that put significance on ideal and responsive correspondence.

The stage's prosperity is likewise clear in its capacity to explore the test of contrasting social mentalities toward progressive connections and customs. WhatsApp's openness and familiarity appeal to a wide client base, yet the stage likewise perceives social varieties in correspondence styles. For example, in societies where customs are underscored, people can address each other with titles and regard formal language shows inside the informing connection point.

WhatsApp's progress in various semantic and social settings reaches out past individual clients to incorporate organizations and associations. The stage's joining of business highlights, like WhatsApp Business and WhatsApp Business Programming interface, recognizes the assorted manners by which organizations work all around the world. The capacity to manage deals, client care, and promoting through a recognizable and broadly utilized informing stage lines up with social assumptions for comfort and openness.

The outcome of WhatsApp in various etymological and social settings is likewise intently attached to the stage's reaction to nearby requirements and difficulties. For example, in locales with restricted web network, WhatsApp's enhancement for low-data transmission conditions guarantees a consistent client experience. This flexibility to assorted mechanical frameworks adds to the stage's prominence in regions where web access might be irregular or obliged.

WhatsApp's prosperity is set apart by its responsiveness to social awarenesses and administrative structures. In certain areas, where social standards direct limitations on specific kinds of content or correspondence, WhatsApp has executed elements, for example, bunch administrator controls and detailing systems to enable clients to deal with their computerized spaces in arrangement with nearby social assumptions.

WhatsApp's effect on political and municipal commitment shifts across social and topographical settings. In locales where political conversations and activism happen overwhelmingly through computerized channels, WhatsApp fills in as an essential stage for preparation and data spread. Nonetheless, the stage's start to finish encryption and confidential gathering highlights have likewise brought worries up in settings where the spread of deception or radical substance might happen past the domain of public examination.

The progress of WhatsApp in various semantic and social settings is joined with the difficulties presented by falsehood and disinformation. The stage's start to finish encryption, while improving protection, additionally presents difficulties in the recognition and alleviation of misleading data. WhatsApp has executed measures, for example, sending cutoff points and associations with truth actually taking a look at associations to address these difficulties, mirroring a continuous obligation to adjust to the developing scene of computerized correspondence.

WhatsApp's prosperity is additionally molded by its commitment with nearby networks and its responsiveness to client input. The stage effectively looks for input from clients through beta testing programs, client gatherings, and direct criticism systems. This iterative way to deal with improvement guarantees that WhatsApp remains receptive to the advancing requirements and inclinations of its assorted client base, adding to its supported progress in various semantic and social settings.

The effect of WhatsApp's prosperity stretches out to its job in forming computerized ways of behaving and correspondence standards in different social settings. The stage has become necessary to social ceremonies, family correspondence, and expert cooperations in numerous districts. WhatsApp's capacity to flawlessly mix into the texture of day to day existence addresses its social flexibility and its acknowledgment of the focal job correspondence plays in forming and reflecting social personalities.

WhatsApp's progress in various semantic and social settings additionally crosses with the more extensive talk on computerized consideration. The stage's accessibility in various dialects, support for assorted correspondence styles, and thought of differing levels of advanced education add to its part in connecting computerized isolates. WhatsApp fills in as a device for interfacing people who might have restricted admittance to different types of computerized correspondence, in this way adding to social consideration and network.

6.2 Studies of its adoption in various regions

The reception of innovation is a complicated and diverse peculiarity, molded by a bunch of variables including social, financial, and social settings. The investigations of WhatsApp's reception in different districts give significant bits of knowledge into the elements of innovation reception and the manners by which clients from various areas of the planet draw in with this well known informing stage. Looking at these investigations enlightens examples, patterns, and difficulties related with WhatsApp reception, adding to a more profound comprehension of the worldwide effect of this specialized device.

Concentrates on WhatsApp reception frequently start by investigating the elements affecting the choice of clients to embrace the stage. Social elements assume a huge part in forming client inclinations, and studies have reliably featured the significance of social setting in deciding the reception examples of WhatsApp. For instance, in individualistic societies where individual articulation is esteemed, the stage's elements that empower self-articulation, for example, notices and sight and sound sharing, may reverberate emphatically. On the other hand, in collectivist societies, where bunch union is underscored, the stage's gathering informing elements and capacity to work with social coordination become key drivers of reception.

Monetary factors additionally arise as powerful determinants of WhatsApp reception. Concentrates frequently explore the reasonableness of cell phones, the accessibility of portable information plans, and the expense viability of involving WhatsApp for correspondence. In districts where versatile information is costly or cell phones are less common, the reception of WhatsApp might be impacted by the stage's information productivity and low transmission capacity necessities. WhatsApp's underlying obligation to being without promotion and its negligible information utilization added to its allure in locales where information costs are a critical thought for clients.

The job of informal communities and friend impact is a common subject in investigations of WhatsApp reception. The stage's reception frequently follows a viral example, with clients acquainting their contacts with the stage. Studies dig into the systems of social impact, looking at how suggestions from companions, relatives, or partners influence the choice to embrace WhatsApp. The stage's accentuation on associating clients with their current contacts, worked with by highlights like contact synchronization, further enhances the impact of informal organizations in driving reception.

Social standards around correspondence protection and the longing for secure informing stages are subjects of examination in examinations looking at WhatsApp reception. The stage's execution of start to finish encryption, guaranteeing that main the source and beneficiary can get to the substance of messages, lines up with protection assumptions in societies where classified correspondence is exceptionally esteemed. Concentrates frequently investigate how impression of protection and the requirement for secure correspondence impact the reception of WhatsApp over other informing options.

Geological contemplations, like metropolitan provincial partitions and local varieties in web framework, additionally shape the examples of WhatsApp reception. Concentrates on feature how the stage's openness in regions with restricted web network adds to its prominence in provincial or creating areas. The capacity of WhatsApp to work actually in low-data transmission conditions and its moderate plan that takes special care of different mechanical foundations improve its allure in districts with shifting degrees of computerized framework advancement.

Social mentalities toward innovation and advancement are investigated in examinations that explore WhatsApp reception. In certain areas, where mechanical suspicion or protection from change exists, concentrates on look to comprehend the elements that conquer such hindrances and drive the reception of WhatsApp. These elements might incorporate the apparent handiness of the stage, positive client encounters, and the steady acknowledgment of innovation as an indispensable piece of day to day existence.

Language inclinations and etymological variety are focal subjects in investigations of WhatsApp reception. The stage's help for many dialects adds to its inclusivity and wide allure. Concentrates frequently look at the phonetic elements inside WhatsApp discussions, investigating how clients explore multilingual connections, code-exchanging among dialects, and communicating social subtleties through language. The semantic flexibility of WhatsApp assumes a pivotal part in its prosperity across different phonetic scenes.

Diverse examinations dig into the manners by which WhatsApp is adjusted and coordinated into various social correspondence rehearses. These investigations investigate how clients from different social foundations utilize WhatsApp highlights for various purposes, for example, keeping up with social associations, planning bunch exercises, or managing deals.

The flexibility of WhatsApp to different social standards and correspondence styles is a typical subject in multifaceted examinations.

Fleeting parts of WhatsApp reception, including the development of client ways of behaving over the long haul, are subjects of examination in longitudinal investigations. These examinations track the progressions in client commitment, highlight use, and correspondence designs on the stage overstretched periods. Longitudinal examination gives bits of knowledge into how WhatsApp adjusts to developing client needs, mechanical progressions, and changes in social elements.

Social and political elements of WhatsApp reception are investigated in examinations that research the stage's part in molding public talk, political commitment, and social developments. The spread of data, deception, and the elements of data stream inside WhatsApp bunches become central places of request. Concentrates frequently address the ramifications of the stage's start to finish encryption for issues connected with data legitimacy, responsibility, and the difficulties of content balance in confidential social scenes.

Concentrates likewise look at segment varieties in WhatsApp reception, taking into account factors like age, orientation, and financial status. The inclinations and use examples of various segment bunches give nuanced experiences into the different manners by which WhatsApp is incorporated into individuals' lives. For instance, more youthful clients might use the stage for mingling and media sharing, while more established clients might focus on its utility for family correspondence and coordination.

Client fulfillment and the elements affecting client maintenance are subjects of interest in examinations that assess the drawn out effect of WhatsApp reception. These examinations investigate client encounters, include inclinations, and the purposes for supported commitment with the stage. Factors like the unwavering quality of informing administrations, usability, and the responsiveness of the stage to client criticism add to client fulfillment and assume a pivotal part in the supported outcome of WhatsApp.

Concentrates likewise address difficulties related with WhatsApp reception, including issues of falsehood, protection concerns, and the potential for the stage to be abused for malignant purposes. The stage's reactions to these difficulties, like the presentation of sending limits, instructive drives, and coordinated efforts with reality actually looking at associations, are examined with regards to client discernments and the more extensive cultural effect of WhatsApp.

6.3 The role of language support and cultural sensitivity

The job of language support and social responsiveness in innovation, especially correspondence stages like WhatsApp, is a basic perspective that significantly impacts client experience, reception, and the stage's effect across different worldwide networks.

Analyzing the interchange between language support, social awareness, and the progress of correspondence stages divulges bits of knowledge into the intricacies of taking care of different etymological and social settings. As computerized correspondence turns out to be progressively basic to our lives, understanding how language and social elements shape the plan and reception of these stages is fundamental.

Language support remains at the front of contemplations for correspondence stages looking for worldwide importance. The capacity to convey in one's local language encourages inclusivity and guarantees that people from different etymological foundations can connect easily with the stage. WhatsApp's obligation to multilingualism is clear in its help for an immense range of dialects, from broadly spoken ones to provincial and minority dialects. This comprehensive methodology recognizes the phonetic variety of its client base and mirrors a comprehension of the significance of language in molding social character.

The job of language support stretches out past the simple arrangement of a multilingual point of interaction. Correspondence stages that genuinely focus on semantic variety put resources into precise and socially touchy language interpretation. This includes deciphering UIs as well as guaranteeing that substance, messages, and other correspondence components are precisely conveyed in various dialects. Socially delicate interpretation considers etymological subtleties, colloquial articulations, and social setting, adding to a more genuine and interesting client experience.

For WhatsApp, the meaning of language support goes past empowering individual clients to explore the stage in their favored language. The stage's obligation to multilingual correspondence inside discussions is a demonstration of its acknowledgment of the phonetic elements of multicultural social orders. Clients can consistently switch between dialects inside a solitary talk, mirroring the liquid and multilingual nature of genuine discussions. This element not just obliges clients who explore between various dialects in their everyday correspondence yet additionally supports the stage's versatility to assorted phonetic settings.

The progress of correspondence stages in encouraging worldwide associations is complicatedly connected to their capacity to rise above language hindrances. Highlights that work with cross-lingual correspondence, like continuous interpretation, add to the inclusivity of these stages. WhatsApp, while not offering constant interpretation inside the application, permits clients to impart in different dialects inside a visit.

This adaptability lines up with the multilingual real factors of numerous clients and accentuates the stage's obligation to separating language hindrances in advanced correspondence.

Social responsiveness, firmly entwined with language support, assumes a significant part in molding the client experience on correspondence stages. Social responsiveness goes past language interpretation to include a profound comprehension of social standards, social practices, and awarenesses. Stages that focus on social responsiveness recognize the assorted manners by which clients from various social foundations draw in with innovation and correspondence.

The plan of UIs mirrors the social responsiveness of correspondence stages. Contemplations, for example, variety plans, images, and design structures are adjusted to line up with social feel and inclinations. WhatsApp's moderate and natural plan, described by effectively reasonable symbols and a clear talk format, mirrors a general methodology that rises above social contrasts. This effortlessness adds to the stage's availability across various social settings, taking special care of clients with differing levels of mechanical commonality.

Social responsiveness is likewise obvious in the consolidation of socially applicable substance inside correspondence stages. This reaches out to the accessibility of pictures, representations, and mixed media components that mirror the social variety of clients. Stages that curate satisfied with aversion to social standards and variety enhance the client experience as well as add to a feeling of inclusivity. The portrayal of different social characters in visual components cultivates a positive impression of the stage as one that qualities and regards the social foundations of its clients.

The versatility of correspondence stages to different social correspondence styles is a critical component of social responsiveness. Various societies might have unmistakable inclinations in regards to correspondence standards, custom, and certainty. Stages that perceive and oblige these varieties in correspondence styles are better situated to work with significant communications. For instance, in societies where customs are accentuated, correspondence stages might consolidate highlights that permit clients to address each other with titles and regard formal language shows.

WhatsApp's progress in various social settings is set apart by its versatility to nearby correspondence standards. The presentation of highlights like notices, which permit clients to convey their mind-set or offer updates inside the stage, mirrors a comprehension of the assorted manners by which people put themselves out there. The fuse of emoticons, stickers, and GIFs, which rise above language boundaries and empower expressive correspondence, reverberates with clients across various societies. These visual components give an all inclusive language that adds a layer of lavishness to computerized discussions, encouraging a feeling of association and understanding.

Accepted practices around security and the plan of correspondence stages are likewise formed by social contemplations. WhatsApp's execution of start to finish encryption, guaranteeing the secrecy of client messages, lines up with protection assumptions in societies where private correspondence is profoundly esteemed. Studies have shown that in districts where protection concerns are vital, the reception of WhatsApp is affected by the stage's obligation to get and confidential correspondence. The stage's accentuation on client security adds to dependability according to clients focus on the assurance of their own data.

Geological and provincial subtleties are vital parts of social responsiveness in correspondence stages. Stages that think about provincial varieties in friendly practices, occasions, and far-reaching developments can tailor elements to line up with these particular settings. For instance, WhatsApp's consolidation of highlights like Diwali-themed stickers or Chinese New Year livelinesss mirrors a consciousness of comprehensive developments and merriments that resound with clients in unambiguous districts. By recognizing and celebrating social variety, correspondence stages add to a feeling of local area and having a place among clients.

The versatility of correspondence stages to social awarenesses is especially significant with regards to arising advances like computerized reasoning (simulated intelligence) and augmented reality (VR). Computer based intelligence calculations that power suggestion frameworks and content curation should be prepared on different datasets that record for social varieties. Predisposition in simulated intelligence calculations can propagate social generalizations and add to imbalances in satisfied portrayal. Social awareness in man-made intelligence advancement includes thinking about the different viewpoints, values, and standards present in the client base.

Computer generated reality, with its vivid nature, offers open doors for social encounters and associations. Socially delicate VR applications can ship clients to virtual conditions that reflect assorted social settings, verifiable settings, and imaginative articulations. Nonetheless, designers should move toward social portrayal with care to keep away from social allotment, distortion, or the support of generalizations. The moral contemplations of social awareness stretch out to the capable creation and utilization of virtual spaces that regard the social personalities of clients.

The worldwide progress of correspondence stages is dependent upon their capacity to explore the difficulties related with social variety. One such test is the potential for misconception or confusion of messages because of social contrasts in correspondence styles or etymological subtleties. Stages that consolidate highlights to moderate these difficulties, for example, continuous interpretation or social responsiveness preparing for man-made intelligence calculations, exhibit a pledge to upgrading diverse correspondence.

The effect of language support and social awareness stretches out past individual clients to incorporate organizations, associations, and different areas. In the business domain, correspondence stages that offer multilingual help and social versatility are significant for worldwide joint efforts, client communications, and market outreach. The capacity to convey actually across phonetic and social limits adds to the outcome of worldwide undertakings.

The medical care area, where successful correspondence is central, benefits from correspondence stages that think about language variety and social subtleties. Telemedicine stages, for instance, should guarantee that language support obliges different patient populaces. Social responsiveness in medical care correspondence stages reaches out to the arrangement of wellbeing data, patient schooling materials, and the thought of social inclinations in medical services communications.

Chapter 7

Strategic Integrations and Partnerships

In the quickly developing scene of business and innovation, the job of key mixes and associations has become progressively imperative for associations planning to flourish in the perplexing and interconnected worldwide commercial center. The conventional worldview of independent substances working in segregation has given way to a more cooperative and synergistic methodology, where key mixes and organizations act as the key part for development, development, and manageability.

At the core of this shift is the acknowledgment that no association has a restraining infrastructure on mastery, assets, or market access. In a period described by exceptional mechanical progressions and sped up globalization, organizations are constrained to investigate cooperative techniques that influence corresponding qualities and encourage an aggregate way to deal with critical thinking. The essential mix of divergent components, whether it be innovations, business cycles, or ability, has arisen as a key empowering influence for associations looking to explore the intricacies of the cutting edge business scene.

One conspicuous impetus of key mixes is the constant speed of mechanical development. As mechanical leap forwards happen at a surprising rate, associations are tested to remain on the ball or chance out of date quality. Vital combinations with innovation accomplices offer a way to take advantage of state of the art progressions without the weight of in-house improvement. Whether through consolidations, acquisitions, or cooperative endeavors, organizations are progressively shaping unions that permit them to tackle the force of arising innovations like man-made brainpower, blockchain, and quantum registering.

Besides, the journey for readiness and versatility even with dynamic economic situations has moved associations towards key organizations for the purpose of upgrading adaptability. The capacity to answer quickly to changes in purchaser inclinations, administrative scenes, or serious elements is vital for keeping up with importance and upper hand. Through essential associations, associations can pool assets, share chances, and explore vulnerability more actually than if they somehow managed to go solo.

The idea of vital organizations stretches out past the domain of innovation to incorporate a range of cooperative plans that length ventures and areas. In a globalized economy, the essential joining of supply chains has turned into an essential basic for associations trying to upgrade effectiveness and relieve gambles.

By fashioning organizations with providers, producers, and merchants, organizations can make a consistent and versatile store network that is better prepared to endure disturbances and vacillations popular.

The essential incorporation of assorted ability pools is one more feature of cooperative procedures that associations are progressively utilizing. Perceiving that development is in many cases a consequence of different points of view and ranges of abilities, organizations are framing associations with instructive establishments, research associations, and even contenders to get to a more extensive ability environment. This not just cultivates a culture of persistent learning and development yet in addition tends to the developing interest for particular abilities in a steadily developing position market.

Key incorporations and associations are tied in with getting to outside capacities as well as about opening collaborations inside associations. As organizations grow their tasks and expand their item or administration portfolios, the requirement for inner cooperation becomes fundamental. Siloed divisions and divided correspondence channels can block effectiveness and impede the acknowledgment of vital goals. Associations are, in this way, putting resources into coordinated frameworks, cooperative stages, and cross-practical groups to encourage a culture of inner participation and shared objectives.

The monetary ramifications of vital combinations and organizations are a basic thought for associations exploring this landscape. While the advantages of joint effort are apparent, the expenses and dangers related with reconciliation can't be disregarded. Consolidations and acquisitions, for example, require fastidious reasonable level of investment to survey the similarity of hierarchical societies, frameworks, and cycles. The inability to deal with these elements successfully can bring about combination challenges, worker separation, and monetary misfortunes.

To moderate these dangers, associations are embracing an essential way to deal with organizations that goes past prompt monetary benefits. Instead of zeroing in exclusively on transient returns, organizations are putting accentuation on adjusting vital goals, values, and long haul dreams with their accomplices. This shift towards an additional comprehensive and forward-looking point of view is obvious in the ascent of direction driven associations, where associations meet up to address cultural difficulties, advance maintainability, and add to the prosperity of networks.

The approach of Industry 4.0, described by the combination of advanced innovations, large information, and the Web of Things (IoT), has additionally sped up the requirement for vital reconciliations and organizations. As businesses go through advanced changes, the limits between areas obscure, leading to new environments where cooperation isn't simply favorable however basic.

Associations are framing unions with players from assorted ventures to co-make inventive arrangements, share information bits of knowledge, and investigate new plans of action that gain by the interconnectedness of current advances.

The essential coordination of information is a focal topic in the time of computerized change. With information arising as a significant cash, associations are looking for ways of opening maximum capacity through organizations work with consistent information sharing and examination. Information joint efforts, be that as it may, deliver complex difficulties connected with protection, security, and administrative consistence. Subsequently, associations participating in such organizations should explore a scene laden with lawful and moral contemplations, requiring a sensitive harmony among transparency and security.

In the domain of medical services, the essential combination of information and advancements is reshaping the scene of patient consideration and clinical exploration. Organizations between medical services suppliers, innovation organizations, and examination foundations are cultivating developments like customized medication, distant patient observing, and prescient investigation. These joint efforts upgrade the nature of medical care conveyance as well as add to the progression of clinical science and the advancement of cutting edge therapies.

The essential joining of manageability rehearses has arisen as a principal quality of contemporary business organizations. With a developing accentuation on corporate social obligation and natural stewardship, associations are looking for accomplices who share a promise to feasible practices. Joint efforts that attention on diminishing carbon impressions, advancing round economies, and tending to social disparities are acquiring unmistakable quality, driven by the acknowledgment that drawn out progress is indistinguishable from dependable and moral strategic policies.

The advancement of vital combinations and associations isn't without its difficulties. The intricacies of overseeing different partners, adjusting unique interests, and exploring the complexities of worldwide business sectors request a refined way to deal with cooperation. Powerful initiative, clear correspondence, and a common vision are fundamental parts of effective organizations. Associations should likewise be lithe and versatile, fit for recalibrating procedures in light of advancing conditions and arising potential open doors.

All in all, the scene of business in the 21st century is characterized by the essential combinations and organizations that associations produce to explore the intricacies of a quickly developing worldwide climate. Whether driven by mechanical headways, the journey for dexterity, or the basic of manageability, cooperative techniques have turned into a foundation of progress.

The capacity to saddle the aggregate qualities of different substances, both interior and outside, is a vital differentiator in a period where the speed of progress gives no indications of lessening. As associations keep on embracing the ethos of cooperation, key combinations and organizations will stay significant in molding the eventual fate of business and development.

7.1 Overview of WhatsApp's integration with Facebook-owned platforms

The mix of WhatsApp with different Facebook-claimed stages denotes a huge improvement in the steadily developing scene of web-based entertainment and correspondence advances. WhatsApp, a generally utilized informing application known for its straightforwardness and start to finish encryption, turned into a piece of the Facebook environment after its obtaining in 2014. Throughout the long term, Facebook has decisively sought after the coordination of WhatsApp with its different stages, like Facebook itself and Instagram, determined to make a more durable and interconnected client experience.

One of the essential inspirations driving the incorporation is the craving to smooth out correspondence across stages. Facebook imagines a consistent and bound together insight for clients, permitting them to discuss easily with contacts no matter what the particular stage they are utilizing. This reconciliation goes past simple comfort; it lines up with the more extensive pattern in the tech business towards making bound together biological systems that offer a scope of administrations inside a solitary, interconnected structure.

A vital part of this reconciliation includes cross-stage informing. Facebook has been pursuing empowering clients on WhatsApp to speak with those on Facebook Courier and Instagram Direct. This interoperability is intended to separate the storehouses between these informing administrations, permitting clients to interface with loved ones across various applications without the requirement for different records or the bother of exchanging between stages. This approach is essential for a more extensive procedure to save clients inside the Facebook biological system for longer periods, improving client commitment and making a more exhaustive client profile.

The coordination of WhatsApp with Facebook-claimed stages additionally stretches out to the domain of business correspondence. WhatsApp Business, a variant of the application custom fitted for little and medium-sized undertakings, has been coordinated with Facebook Business Devices. This mix means to furnish organizations with a bound together stage for dealing with their correspondence and client cooperations. By interfacing WhatsApp Business with the more extensive set-up of Facebook Business Instruments, including promoting and client support highlights, organizations can make a more durable and proficient client commitment procedure.

The mix endeavors are not restricted to informing and business correspondence. Facebook has investigated ways of adjusting the foundation of WhatsApp to its different stages, advancing asset use and upgrading the general exhibition of these administrations.

This remembers utilizing Facebook's innovation and ability for regions like substance conveyance, server foundation, and information the board to work on the dependability and versatility of WhatsApp. By sharing assets and innovations across stages, Facebook looks to make a more hearty and strong environment equipped for dealing with the steadily developing requests of a worldwide client base.

While the mix of WhatsApp with Facebook-possessed stages offers a few expected benefits, it has likewise raised concerns connected with client security and information insurance. WhatsApp has been known for its obligation to start to finish encryption, guaranteeing that messages traded on the stage stay private and secure. Notwithstanding, the combination with other Facebook administrations has provoked examination from protection advocates and administrative bodies. The consistent progression of information across stages has started banters about the degree to which client data is shared and the way things are used inside the more extensive Facebook environment.

In light of these worries, Facebook has accentuated its obligation to keeping up with the protection and security includes that clients esteem in WhatsApp. The organization has expressed that start to finish encryption will stay a major part of WhatsApp's personality, even as it incorporates with different administrations. Facebook means to find some kind of harmony between giving a brought together client experience and regarding the protection assumptions for WhatsApp clients. Nonetheless, accomplishing this equilibrium requires cautious route of administrative scenes and progressing endeavors to address arising security worries in the always changing advanced climate.

The mix of WhatsApp with Facebook-claimed stages has likewise acquainted new open doors for organizations with arrive at their ideal interest groups. With the combination of WhatsApp Business and Facebook Business Devices, organizations can make a more firm promoting and client commitment system. The capacity to flawlessly change clients from virtual entertainment stages to private informing for business connections offers a useful asset for client procurement and relationship the executives. Organizations can use the consolidated reach of Facebook, Instagram, and WhatsApp to interface with clients at different touchpoints along their computerized venture.

The incorporation endeavors have not been without challenges. Specialized intricacies, administrative obstacles, and client obstruction are among the elements that organizations should explore as they look to make a fit client experience across stages. Accomplishing genuine interoperability and a consistent client experience requires tending to specialized subtleties, guaranteeing information security consistence, and effectively answering client input. Also, organizations should think about the social and territorial varieties in client inclinations and administrative systems, fitting their joining procedures to assorted crowds.

Looking forward, the incorporation of WhatsApp with Facebook-claimed stages is probably going to keep advancing as innovation, client assumptions, and administrative scenes develop. Facebook's obligation to making a bound together biological system proposes that future improvements might include further incorporation, new elements, and upgraded joint effort between the various administrations under its umbrella. As the computerized scene keeps on moving, the progress of these combination endeavors will rely upon the capacity to adjust to evolving conditions, address arising difficulties, and focus on client trust and protection.

7.2 Analysis of strategic partnerships contributing to its global reach

The examination of key associations uncovers their crucial job in catapulting associations to worldwide reach and impact. In a time characterized by interconnected markets and quick mechanical progressions, organizations progressively perceive the basic of cooperation to explore intricacies, profit by collaborations, and access new roads for development. The essential organizations manufactured by associations go past simple partnerships; they address dynamic biological systems where shared assets, skill, and market access join to make an aggregate effect that rises above individual capacities.

At the center of vital associations is the quest for worldwide reach. Organizations perceive that to flourish in a serious scene, they should broaden their impact past customary limits. Key associations act as an entryway to worldwide business sectors, furnishing associations with the necessary resources to explore administrative scenes, social subtleties, and different purchaser ways of behaving. The pooling of assets, skill, and market bits of knowledge through organizations empowers organizations to lay out a worldwide impression more proficiently than if they somehow managed to set out on performance adventures.

Innovation, a powerful driver of globalization, assumes a urgent part in working with key organizations that rise above geological requirements. Computerized stages and correspondence advances have destroyed conventional obstructions, empowering associations to flawlessly interface with likely accomplices across the globe. Thus, organizations can investigate cooperative open doors, arrange arrangements, and execute joint endeavors with accomplices from various mainlands, cultivating a degree of network and coordinated effort that was once incomprehensible.

One remarkable area where key associations are instrumental in accomplishing worldwide reach is the innovation business. Tech organizations perceive that advancement and market initiative frequently depend on admittance to assorted ability pools and state of the art innovations. Vital organizations empower innovation firms to team up with new companies, research foundations, and other industry players, encouraging a climate of open development. This cooperative methodology speeds up the improvement of new innovations as well as furnishes organizations with a worldwide viewpoint on arising patterns and market requests.

Moreover, the essential organizations framed in the innovation area are not restricted to explicit item advancement drives. They stretch out to regions like cross-permitting of licensed innovation, joint innovative work endeavors, and cooperative endeavors in arising fields like man-made reasoning and quantum registering. These multi-layered organizations contribute not exclusively to the worldwide reach of individual organizations yet in addition to the progression of whole businesses, forming the mechanical scene on a worldwide scale.

The medical services industry additionally represents the effect of vital associations on accomplishing worldwide reach. Given the perplexing idea of medical services frameworks, the variety of administrative structures, and the steady requirement for development, associations in this area are progressively going to organizations to upgrade their worldwide presence. Drug organizations, for example, structure key partnerships with research foundations and biotechnology firms to reinforce their medication revelation and improvement pipelines.

Worldwide arrive at in medical services isn't exclusively about market access; it additionally includes tending to worldwide wellbeing challenges cooperatively. Vital organizations in this area frequently reach out past conventional business coordinated efforts to envelop drives pointed toward further developing medical care foundation, tending to irresistible sicknesses, and propelling general wellbeing objectives. The capacity to produce associations with states, non-benefit associations, and worldwide offices permits medical organizations to add to worldwide wellbeing results while growing their scope and effect.

With regards to maintainability and ecological stewardship, key organizations are demonstrating instrumental in tending to worldwide difficulties, for example, environmental change and asset consumption. Organizations perceive that supportability is an aggregate liability that rises above individual financial matters. Vital organizations in the domain of manageability include joint efforts on eco-accommodating practices, environmentally friendly power drives, and round economy projects.

By combining efforts with similar accomplices, associations can intensify the effect of their manageability drives, driving positive change on a worldwide scale. The worldwide arrive at accomplished through these organizations isn't just about growing portion of the overall industry; it is about on the whole adding to an additional practical and versatile future. As shoppers progressively focus on ecologically cognizant items and practices, vital organizations zeroed in on manageability become an essential basic as well as a market need.

The auto business gives one more focal point through which to examine the job of vital organizations in accomplishing worldwide reach. With the fast advancement of electric and independent vehicles, car organizations are participating in associations to remain at the front of development and market patterns.

Key partnerships between conventional automakers, innovation organizations, and electric vehicle new companies empower cooperative innovative work, shared interests in foundation, and the formation of collaborations that drive the business forward.

Notwithstanding innovation driven associations, car organizations are framing key coalitions to address the worldwide idea of their stock chains and market presence.

Coordinated efforts between automakers from various locales empower them to take advantage of new business sectors, share fabricating capacities, and explore territorial inclinations and guidelines all the more really. These associations are vital for accessing different business sectors as well as for advancing creation processes and accomplishing economies of scale.

Be that as it may, the outcome of key organizations in accomplishing worldwide reach isn't ensured. Associations should explore a horde of difficulties, going from social contrasts and administrative intricacies to different strategic policies and correspondence boundaries. The capacity to adjust vital targets, cultivate compelling correspondence, and fabricate common trust is critical for the outcome of worldwide organizations. Social knowledge and flexibility become fundamental qualities for pioneers guiding associations through the perplexing scene of global joint efforts.

Besides, the changing international scene presents an extra layer of intricacy to worldwide organizations. Moving exchange elements, international strains, and developing administrative conditions require a proactive and deft methodology from associations participated in cross-line joint efforts. The capacity to expect and explore international difficulties turns into a basic skill for organizations looking to outfit the advantages of vital associations in a worldwide setting.

The legitimate and legally binding parts of vital associations additionally request careful consideration. Creating arrangements that obviously characterize jobs, obligations, and assumptions is fundamental for alleviating gambles and guaranteeing the life span of the organization. Disagreements regarding licensed innovation, income sharing systems, or changes in economic situations can endanger the progress of a worldwide association in the event that not tended to through far reaching and very much organized arrangements.

Additionally, the speed of innovative change acquaints a component of vulnerability with key organizations. In ventures driven by quick development, accomplices should be ready to adjust to arising advances, market disturbances, and changing buyer inclinations. Adaptability and an eagerness to develop the terms of cooperation are key credits that associations should develop to flourish in unique ventures and outfit the maximum capacity of worldwide organizations.

As associations explore the complexities of key organizations for worldwide reach, they should likewise be sensitive to the moral components of cooperation. Moral contemplations become progressively significant as organizations draw in with accomplices from different social and administrative foundations.

Issues connected with information security, natural effect, and corporate social obligation require a common obligation to moral strategic policies to guarantee that the advantages of worldwide organizations are offset with capable lead.

7.3 The synergies that enhance user experience across platforms

In the contemporary computerized scene, the idea of cooperative energy becomes the dominant focal point as associations endeavor to make consistent and interconnected client encounters across stages. The expression "collaboration" alludes to the connection or participation of different parts, delivering a joined outcome more prominent than the amount of their different endeavors. When applied to client encounters across stages, collaboration turns into a main thrust behind the reconciliation of innovations, administrations, and points of interaction to upgrade client fulfillment, commitment, and by and large fulfillment.

An essential part of collaborations improving client experience across stages is the coordination of innovations. In this present reality where clients flawlessly change among gadgets and applications, the capacity to synchronize and coordinate innovations turns into a key differentiator. For example, distributed computing assumes a significant part in working with information synchronization, permitting clients to get to their data consistently from different gadgets. Whether a client begins an undertaking on a PC, proceeds with it on a tablet, and afterward finishes it on a cell phone, the hidden collaboration of cloud-based innovations guarantees a reliable and liquid experience.

Also, the reconciliation of computerized reasoning (artificial intelligence) and AI advances contributes essentially to the upgrade of client encounters. These advances, when synergistically applied across stages, empower customized proposals, prescient investigation, and smart computerization. For instance, a client's inclinations and ways of behaving on a streaming stage can be utilized to present custom fitted substance proposals inside the streaming application as well as across related stages, making a strong and customized client venture.

Online entertainment stages represent how cooperative energies across interfaces add to an advanced client experience. The combination of sharing elements permits clients to consistently post content from different applications to their online entertainment profiles. This interconnectedness upgrades client commitment by making a brought together sharing experience across stages, building up a feeling of progression in the client's computerized cooperations. The collaboration between various applications inside the virtual entertainment biological system additionally works with cross-stage correspondence, empowering clients to interface with their contacts no matter what the particular web-based entertainment stage they are utilizing.

Internet business stages, as well, profit by cooperative energies to streamline client encounters. The incorporation of installment entryways, request global positioning frameworks, and customized proposals makes a consistent excursion for clients, from item revelation to buy and then some. By fitting these components across stages, online business suppliers cultivate client steadfastness and fulfillment. The collaboration reaches out to organizations with coordinated factors and installment specialist co-ops, guaranteeing a smooth start to finish insight for clients across different touchpoints.

The combination of increased reality (AR) and augmented reality (VR) innovations addresses one more component of cooperative energies that improve client encounters. Coordinating AR and VR across stages furnishes clients with vivid and reliable encounters, whether they are getting to content through portable applications, sites, or committed AR/VR gadgets. This collaboration stretches out past diversion, finding applications in businesses like retail, training, and medical services, where a strong AR/VR experience improves client commitment and communication.

Cooperative devices and efficiency suites feature the significance of collaborations for clients exploring proficient and individual errands across stages. The consistent combination of record altering, document sharing, and specialized devices guarantees a bound together and effective work process. Whether clients access these apparatuses from a PC, a tablet, or a cell phone, the hidden cooperative energy guarantees that changes made in one connection point are reflected across all stages progressively, encouraging coordinated effort and efficiency.

The domain of computerized content creation additionally profits by cooperative energies across stages. Content makers frequently utilize a blend of instruments, from visual depiction programming to video altering applications. Collaborations between these devices empower smooth changes and interoperability, permitting makers to consistently move their work across various stages. For example, a visual depiction project began a work area application can be progressed forward with a tablet or a cell phone, because of the fundamental collaboration that guarantees document similarity and synchronization.

Versatile working frameworks and application environments exemplify the significance of collaborations in making a durable client experience. Whether clients are on iOS or Android, the mix of uses, administrations, and settings across gadgets guarantees a reliable and natural connection point. The collaboration stretches out to application engineers who influence normal systems and plan standards, permitting clients to explore different applications easily. This interoperability upgrades client solace and diminishes the expectation to absorb information while changing between various gadgets.

In any case, the quest for collaborations across stages isn't without its difficulties. Specialized intricacies, similarity issues, and dissimilar plan standards can present obstacles to making consistent client encounters.

Accomplishing genuine cooperative energy requires a comprehensive methodology that thinks about the specialized viewpoints as well as the client's assumptions and inclinations. Besides, associations should adjust the requirement for joining with the basic of saving variety and decision, guaranteeing that clients have the adaptability to tweak their encounters while profiting from collaborations.

Security and protection contemplations add an extra layer of intricacy to the mission for collaborations across stages. As information streams consistently among gadgets and applications, guaranteeing the secrecy and honesty of client data becomes vital. Associations should execute hearty safety efforts and security shields to fabricate trust among clients who share their information with interconnected stages. Finding some kind of harmony among convenience and security is a nonstop test chasing cooperative energies that improve the client experience.

Availability is another basic aspect that associations should consider while going for the gold stages. Clients cooperate with computerized content through a different cluster of gadgets, each with its own arrangement of capacities and imperatives. Guaranteeing that collaborations don't think twice about is basic for making comprehensive client encounters. Planning points of interaction that adjust to various screen sizes, input strategies, and assistive advances is fundamental to oblige clients with assorted necessities and inclinations.

The advancing scene of guidelines and norms additionally impacts the elements of making collaborations across stages. Information security regulations, like the Overall Information Assurance Guideline (GDPR), put accentuation on client assent, straightforwardness, and command over private information. Associations should explore these administrative systems and guarantee that their quest for cooperative energies lines up with the standards of information insurance and protection. Consistence with developing guidelines requires a proactive and versatile way to deal with keep away from legitimate difficulties and reputational gambles.

The client experience across stages isn't exclusively about specialized incorporation; it is likewise about adjusting brand personalities and values. Associations should consider how their image is addressed reliably across various points of interaction and touchpoints. The visual language, tone of correspondence, and generally speaking brand stylish ought to reverberate durably, making a bound together brand insight for clients. This arrangement adds to memorability, trust, and unwaveringness, building up the positive effect of cooperative energies on the client experience.

As associations keep on putting resources into making cooperative energies that improve the client experience across stages, the job of client criticism becomes crucial. Clients are a definitive appointed authorities of the viability of collaborations in addressing their requirements and assumptions.

Gathering and integrating client criticism into the plan and advancement processes is fundamental for refining collaborations and guaranteeing that they really add to an improved and client driven insight.

Chapter 8

Surge in Emerging Markets

In late many years, the worldwide financial scene has seen a noteworthy flood in developing business sectors. These business sectors, when on the fringe of the world economy, have quickly advanced into dynamic players with critical impact and effect. This flood has been filled by a mix of variables, including globalization, mechanical headways, and moving international elements.

One of the vital drivers of the ascent of developing business sectors is the course of globalization. As boundaries to exchange and speculation have been destroyed, these business sectors have become more coordinated into the worldwide economy. This mix has worked with the progression of capital, merchandise, and administrations across borders, setting out new open doors for development and improvement.

Mechanical progressions play had a critical impact in this change. The computerized transformation, specifically, has empowered developing business sectors to jump customary progressive phases. Portable innovation, web availability, and advanced stages have enabled organizations and people in these business sectors, opening up new roads for development and financial support.

The flood in developing business sectors is certainly not a uniform peculiarity, as various locales have encountered fluctuating levels of development and improvement. Asia, for example, has arisen as a force to be reckoned with of financial action, with nations like China, India, and Southeast Asian countries encountering fast industrialization and urbanization. These nations have utilized their huge populaces and plentiful assets to become key part on the worldwide stage.

Africa, as well, has seen huge improvement in specific regions, in spite of the fact that difficulties like framework shortages, political unsteadiness, and social issues keep on presenting impediments to supported development. Latin America, with its different economies, has seen a blended direction, for certain nations making surprising progress while others wrestle with monetary and political vulnerabilities.

The flood in developing business sectors has reshaped the equilibrium of monetary power worldwide. Conventional financial forces to be reckoned with in the West are progressively winding up imparting the stage to dynamic players from the East, South, and different locales. This shift has suggestions for the international scene, as developing business sectors stand up for themselves monetarily as well as strategically.

One eminent part of the ascent of developing business sectors is the job of China. The world's most crowded country has gone through a quick monetary change throughout recent many years, progressing from a fundamentally agrarian culture to a modern and mechanical force to be reckoned with. China's reconciliation into the worldwide economy has been a main thrust behind the flood in developing business sectors, as its interest for unrefined substances, energy, and buyer products has set out open doors for other creating economies.

China's Belt and Street Drive (BRI) epitomizes its essential way to deal with worldwide financial commitment. Through gigantic framework projects, China expects to associate Asia, Europe, and Africa, cultivating financial participation and advancement along these passageways. The BRI has turned into an image of China's desire to shape the monetary eventual fate of not exclusively its locale yet the world overall.

While the flood in developing business sectors presents new open doors for development and improvement, it likewise achieves a large group of difficulties. Financial development in these business sectors has frequently been joined by natural debasement, asset consumption, and social imbalances. Adjusting the goals of monetary advancement with reasonable and comprehensive improvement is a mind boggling task that requires insightful approaches and procedures.

Also, the flood in developing business sectors has suggestions for the worldwide exchanging framework. As these business sectors become more huge players in worldwide exchange, inquiries of fair contest, licensed innovation freedoms, and natural norms come to the cutting edge. The standards based request that has represented worldwide exchange for quite a long time might have to adjust to oblige the different requirements and interests of arising economies.

The monetary area has additionally been significantly impacted by the flood in developing business sectors. The developing monetary clout of these business sectors has prompted expanded interest for monetary administrations, going from banking and protection to venture and abundance the executives. Worldwide monetary establishments and global organizations are recalibrating their procedures to take advantage of the immense capability of these developing business sectors.

The flood in developing business sectors has reshaped the worldwide financial scene as well as significantly affected the existences of millions of individuals. In many emerging nations, enhancements in training, medical care, and foundation have went with monetary development. Notwithstanding, difficulties like destitution, disparity, and admittance to essential administrations continue, featuring the requirement for comprehensive and reasonable improvement systems.

One region where the effect of the flood in developing business sectors is especially obvious is the innovation area. Development center points have arisen in surprising spots, driven by a mix of nearby ability, pioneering soul, and ideal monetary circumstances. New companies in developing business sectors are disturbing customary enterprises, making new plans of action, and adding to the worldwide advancement environment.

The flood in developing business sectors has likewise started a reexamination of customary improvement standards. The thought that financial advancement should follow a direct way, with nations developing through progressive phases, is being tested. Developing business sectors are exhibiting that elective pathways to thriving are conceivable, and that achievement can be accomplished through a mix of financial sober mindedness and social development.

In any case, the flood in developing business sectors isn't without its vulnerabilities. International pressures, exchange debates, and the effect of worldwide occasions, for example, the Coronavirus pandemic can present huge difficulties to the proceeded with development of these business sectors. The interconnected idea of the worldwide economy implies that improvements in a single region of the planet can have sweeping ramifications for developing business sectors as well as the other way around.

All in all, the flood in developing business sectors addresses a groundbreaking power in the worldwide economy. The ascent of dynamic economies in Asia, Africa, Latin America, and different areas is reshaping customary ideas of monetary power and impact. The incorporation of these business sectors into the worldwide economy, worked with by innovative progressions and globalization, has set out new open doors and difficulties.

As developing business sectors keep on advocating for themselves on the world stage, the requirement for cooperative and comprehensive ways to deal with worldwide advancement turns out to be progressively evident. The flood in developing business sectors isn't simply an account of monetary development; a perplexing story includes social, political, and natural aspects. Adjusting the objectives of progress with the standards of maintainability and value is an errand that requires aggregate exertion and smart policymaking. The eventual fate of the worldwide economy will be formed by our decisions today in exploring the intricacies and open doors introduced by the flood in developing business sectors.

8.1 Exploration of WhatsApp's popularity in emerging economies

WhatsApp, an informing application that began as a straightforward text informing stage, has developed into a worldwide correspondence peculiarity with an especially impressive traction in arising economies. This investigation dives into the elements that add to WhatsApp's notoriety in these locales, looking at the financial, mechanical, and social elements that have moved the application to the front of specialized devices.

One of the essential drivers behind WhatsApp's ubiquity in arising economies is its low obstruction to passage. Dissimilar to conventional SMS benefits that frequently cause extra charges, WhatsApp uses web availability for correspondence. This shift from customary informing techniques to web based informing has been particularly worthwhile in districts where admittance to reasonable and dependable portable information has become progressively pervasive.

Moderateness is a urgent figure the far reaching reception of WhatsApp in arising economies. The actual application is allowed to download and utilize, wiping out the requirement for clients to cause extra expenses for fundamental correspondence. This has made WhatsApp an alluring choice for people in locales where financial imperatives might restrict spending on correspondence administrations. The expense viability of involving WhatsApp for instant messages, voice calls, and even video calls plays had a critical impact in its mass allure.

Moreover, WhatsApp's lightweight plan adds to its notoriety in regions where cell phones with restricted capacity and it are pervasive to handle power. The application is streamlined to work flawlessly even on passage level cell phones, making it open to a wide range of clients. This versatility to different mechanical conditions has situated WhatsApp as a go-to correspondence stage for clients across different financial layers in arising economies.

The ascent of WhatsApp in developing business sectors is entwined with the more extensive pattern of expanding web entrance. As additional individuals get close enough to the web, particularly through cell phones, the reception of informing applications like WhatsApp has flooded. The application's easy to use interface, combined with its capacity to work on 2G and 3G organizations, has permitted it to arrive at clients in regions with fluctuating degrees of mechanical foundation.

The nonconcurrent idea of informing on WhatsApp lines up with the correspondence inclinations of clients in arising economies. Not at all like calls that require quick consideration, informing considers greater adaptability in answering, obliging clients with fluctuated everyday schedules and responsibilities. This nonconcurrent correspondence style is especially appropriate for districts where people might have capricious plans for getting work done or restricted admittance to continuous correspondence.

Notwithstanding its specialized elements, WhatsApp's outcome in arising economies is profoundly entwined with the socio-social texture of these districts. Many developing business sectors have solid common ties and a culture of affectionate connections. WhatsApp's gathering talk usefulness takes care of this social perspective, empowering clients to remain associated with family, companions, and local area individuals in a consistent and comprehensive way.

The meaning of WhatsApp in familial and local area associations is clear in its utilization for sharing updates, photographs, and even mixed media content. In districts where family bonds assume a focal part in day to day existence, the application fills in as a virtual social event space, permitting clients to share snapshots of their lives continuously. This common part of WhatsApp lines up with social qualities in many arising economies, further setting its status as a favored specialized device.

Besides, WhatsApp has turned into a center point for business correspondence in developing business sectors, adding to its boundless reception. Little and medium-sized endeavors (SMEs) influence the stage for client communications, request handling, and in any event, advertising. The application's business-accommodating elements, for example, WhatsApp Business, empower endeavors to lay out an immediate line of correspondence with their client base, encouraging trust and dependability.

The comfort presented by WhatsApp Business in taking care of client requests and furnishing ongoing updates resounds with organizations working in asset obliged conditions. This immediate and quick method of correspondence is particularly significant for miniature business visionaries and neighborhood organizations in arising economies, permitting them to conquer conventional obstructions and contend in the computerized commercial center.

Nonetheless, the ascent of WhatsApp in developing business sectors has not been without challenges. The application has confronted investigation for security concerns, particularly as its parent organization, Facebook, coordinates elements and information dividing instruments among stages. In locales where information assurance guidelines might be less severe, clients are progressively becoming mindful of the need to adjust the accommodation of informing applications with the security of their own data.

Besides, the spread of deception and the test of controlling the scattering of bogus or deluding content have been major problems related with WhatsApp in arising economies. The application's start to finish encryption, while guaranteeing security, has additionally made it trying to screen and check the spread of phony news. State run administrations and associations in these locales are wrestling with procedures to resolve this issue and advance computerized proficiency among clients.

Notwithstanding these difficulties, WhatsApp keeps on assuming a urgent part in molding computerized correspondence patterns in arising economies. The application's effect stretches out past private correspondence and business collaborations; it has turned into a stage for community commitment and social preparation. From political missions to local area drives, WhatsApp bunches have turned into a useful asset for sorting out and spreading data.

The instructive area in arising economies has additionally seen the groundbreaking impact of WhatsApp. In districts where conventional methods of training might confront infrastructural challenges, the application has been used for distance learning, educator understudy correspondence, and the sharing of instructive assets. This transformation features the application's flexibility in tending to assorted needs inside advancing financial scenes.

As WhatsApp's prevalence in arising economies keeps on developing, it brings up issues about the ramifications for nearby correspondence environments and the more extensive advanced scene. The application's strength in informing administrations has prompted worries about rivalry and possible monopolistic practices. Also, the joining of installment highlights inside WhatsApp further expands its venture into monetary exchanges, presenting the two valuable open doors and difficulties for the monetary area in these locales.

All in all, the investigation of WhatsApp's prominence in arising economies uncovers a complicated transaction of mechanical, financial, social, and social variables. The application's prosperity isn't only a consequence of its specialized elements yet is well established in its capacity to line up with the different necessities and inclinations of clients in these locales. As WhatsApp proceeds to advance and coordinate new elements, its effect on correspondence, business, and society in arising economies is probably going to stay significant, molding the computerized scene into the indefinite future.

8.2 Factors contributing to its success in regions with diverse economic conditions

The outcome of WhatsApp in districts with different financial circumstances can be credited to a mix of variables that on the whole add to its broad reception and supported fame. These variables envelop mechanical versatility, moderateness, social arrangement, and the application's capacity to address explicit difficulties predominant in financially different conditions.

Mechanical flexibility stands apart as a critical driver of WhatsApp's outcome in districts with different financial circumstances. The application's plan and usefulness are to such an extent that it can work consistently across a range of mechanical conditions, from rapid web associations in metropolitan habitats to additional compelled conditions in rustic regions. This versatility guarantees that WhatsApp stays open to an expansive client base, no matter what the fluctuating degrees of mechanical framework in various locales.

WhatsApp's lightweight nature assumes a significant part in this versatility. Not at all like some asset concentrated applications, WhatsApp is upgraded to work on gadgets with restricted capacity and handling power. This makes it viable with a scope of cell phones, including section level and more seasoned models that might be predominant in financially different locales. Subsequently, clients across various financial layers can draw in with the application without confronting mechanical boundaries.

Moderateness is another basic variable adding to WhatsApp's outcome in financially assorted areas. The actual application is allowed to download and utilize, taking out the requirement for clients to distribute a critical part of their spending plans to correspondence administrations. This is especially significant in locales where monetary imperatives might restrict spending on superfluous administrations. WhatsApp's expense adequacy stretches out past informing to incorporate voice and video calls, making it an appealing choice for those looking for reasonable correspondence options.

The dependence on web network for correspondence is a characterizing element of WhatsApp and a critical calculate its outcome in financially different locales. As admittance to portable information turns out to be more common and reasonable, the application's reliance on web network turns out to be to a lesser extent a boundary. Also, WhatsApp's capacity to work on 2G and 3G organizations guarantees that clients in regions with differing levels of network can in any case draw in with the application, though with possibly decreased speeds.

The socio-social scene of financially different districts assumes a urgent part in WhatsApp's prosperity. The application's elements, for example, bunch talks and mixed media sharing, line up with social standards in a large number of these locales. For instance, in social orders where mutual ties areas of strength for are, bunch talk usefulness permits clients to remain associated with family, companions, and local area individuals in a virtual space. The sharing of updates, photographs, and recordings turns into a method for crossing over topographical distances and keep up with affectionate connections.

In financially different locales, where familial and local area securities frequently outweigh everything else, WhatsApp turns out to be something other than a specialized device — it turns into a virtual social occasion space. This social arrangement improves the application's allure and concretes its job in working with social associations. The significance of WhatsApp in cultivating and keeping up with connections mirrors its consistent mix into the texture of day to day existence in these districts.

Moreover, WhatsApp's prosperity is enhanced by its utilization as a stage for business correspondence in monetarily different conditions. Little and medium-sized undertakings (SMEs) influence the application for client associations, request handling, and promoting.

The application's business-accommodating elements, for example, WhatsApp Business, empower endeavors to lay out an immediate line of correspondence with their client base, cultivating trust and dependability.

The comfort presented by WhatsApp Business in taking care of client requests and furnishing ongoing updates reverberates with organizations working in asset compelled conditions. For miniature business visionaries and nearby organizations in financially assorted areas, WhatsApp evens the odds, permitting them to contend in the advanced commercial center. This part of WhatsApp's prosperity isn't exclusively reliant upon individual clients however reaches out to a more extensive monetary effect, adding to the development of neighborhood organizations.

Regardless of its various benefits, WhatsApp's outcome in financially assorted locales isn't without challenges. Security concerns have arisen as a critical issue, especially considering the application's mix with its parent organization, Facebook. Clients in these locales are progressively becoming mindful of the significance of safeguarding their own data, and worries about information security might impact the application's reception, particularly in districts with developing information assurance guidelines.

One more test related with WhatsApp's ubiquity in monetarily different areas is the spread of deception. The application's start to finish encryption, while guaranteeing protection, has made it trying to screen and control the scattering of bogus or deluding content. Legislatures, associations, and WhatsApp itself have needed to wrestle with systems to resolve this issue and advance computerized education among clients.

Additionally, the combination of installment highlights inside WhatsApp presents the two valuable open doors and difficulties for monetarily assorted districts. While advanced installments can improve monetary consideration and comfort, they likewise bring up issues about security, administrative structures, and the possible grouping of monetary power inside the application. These difficulties require a sensitive harmony among development and guaranteeing the security of clients in districts with different monetary circumstances.

WhatsApp's effect stretches out past private correspondence and business collaborations; it has turned into a stage for municipal commitment and social preparation in financially different districts. From political missions to local area drives, WhatsApp bunches have turned into an integral asset for sorting out and scattering data. This city aspect of WhatsApp mirrors its ability to adjust to the different requirements of clients and networks, adding to social availability and interest.

The instructive area in monetarily assorted locales has additionally encountered the groundbreaking impact of WhatsApp. In regions where customary methods of training face infrastructural challenges, the application has been used for distance learning, educator understudy correspondence, and the sharing of instructive assets. This transformation features the application's flexibility in tending to different requirements inside advancing financial scenes.

As WhatsApp's prevalence keeps on filling in financially different districts, it brings up issues about the ramifications for nearby correspondence environments and the more extensive advanced scene. The application's strength in informing administrations has prompted worries about rivalry and possible monopolistic practices. Moreover, the mix of installment highlights inside WhatsApp further broadens its venture into monetary exchanges, presenting the two open doors and difficulties for the monetary area in these districts.

All in all, the progress of WhatsApp in locales with different monetary circumstances can be credited to a blend of mechanical versatility, reasonableness, social arrangement, and its capacity to address explicit difficulties predominant in these conditions. As WhatsApp proceeds to develop and coordinate new highlights, its effect on correspondence, business, and society in financially different districts is probably going to stay significant, molding the computerized scene into the indefinite future.

8.3 The platform's impact on communication trends in developing nations

WhatsApp's effect on correspondence patterns in non-industrial countries has been groundbreaking, reshaping the way people, organizations, and networks associate and convey. This effect is diverse, including innovative headways, socio-social movements, financial strengthening, and, surprisingly, political and urban commitment. This investigation digs into the different elements of WhatsApp's effect on correspondence in non-industrial countries, looking at the manners by which the stage has turned into a key part of network and cooperation.

One of the most outstanding parts of WhatsApp's effect is its job in beating conventional correspondence hindrances. In many non-industrial countries, admittance to reasonable and dependable correspondence administrations has generally been a test. Customary methods of correspondence, for example, landline telephones and even SMS administrations, frequently caused massive expenses, restricting their availability to specific sections of the populace. WhatsApp, with its web based informing and calling administrations, has democratized correspondence by giving a financially savvy and comprehensive stage.

The moderateness of WhatsApp is a key element adding to its far reaching reception in non-industrial countries. The actual application is allowed to download and utilize, and its utilization of web information for informing and calls disposes of the requirement for clients to spend on customary specialized strategies.

This cost-adequacy is especially huge in locales where monetary imperatives might restrict spending on trivial administrations. WhatsApp's capacity to offer a solid and minimal expense correspondence arrangement has situated it as a favored decision for people and organizations the same.

Besides, WhatsApp's progress in emerging countries is intently attached to the rising accessibility and moderateness of portable information. As portable organizations extend and information costs decline, more individuals in non-industrial countries get sufficiently close to the web. WhatsApp, being a web subordinate stage, benefits from this pattern. The application's versatility to work on 2G and 3G organizations guarantees that clients in regions with shifting degrees of network can in any case draw in with the stage, working with correspondence even in asset obliged conditions.

The nonconcurrent idea of informing on WhatsApp lines up with the correspondence inclinations of clients in non-industrial countries. Dissimilar to calls that request quick consideration, informing considers greater adaptability in answering. This nonconcurrent correspondence style obliges clients with different everyday schedules and responsibilities, mirroring the real factors of life in emerging countries where capricious plans for getting work done and restricted admittance to continuous correspondence might be predominant.

The socio-social elements of non-industrial countries assume a critical part in forming WhatsApp's effect on correspondence. In large numbers of these areas, mutual ties and affectionate connections structure an essential piece of day to day existence. WhatsApp's gathering talk usefulness takes special care of this social viewpoint, empowering clients to remain associated with family, companions, and local area individuals in a virtual space. The sharing of updates, photographs, and recordings turns into a method for crossing over geological distances and keep up with social associations.

Besides, WhatsApp has turned into a center for business correspondence in emerging countries, adding to monetary strengthening. Little and medium-sized undertakings (SMEs) influence the stage for client collaborations, request handling, and advertising. The application's business-accommodating elements, like WhatsApp Business, engage organizations to lay out an immediate line of correspondence with their client base, encouraging trust and faithfulness.

The comfort presented by WhatsApp Business in taking care of client requests and furnishing continuous updates reverberates with organizations working in asset obliged conditions. For miniature business visionaries and neighborhood organizations in agricultural countries, WhatsApp evens the odds, permitting them to contend in the advanced commercial center. This part of WhatsApp's effect isn't exclusively reliant upon individual clients yet reaches out to a more extensive monetary effect, adding to the development of nearby organizations.

In spite of its various benefits, WhatsApp's effect in emerging countries isn't without challenges. Protection concerns have arisen as a critical issue, especially as the application coordinates with its parent organization, Facebook. Clients in these districts are turning out to be progressively mindful of the significance of safeguarding their own data, and worries about information security might impact the application's reception, particularly in locales with advancing information assurance guidelines.

One more test related with WhatsApp's fame in non-industrial countries is the spread of deception. The application's start to finish encryption, while guaranteeing protection, has made it trying to screen and control the spread of bogus or deceiving content. State run administrations, associations, and WhatsApp itself have needed to wrestle with systems to resolve this issue and advance computerized proficiency among clients.

In addition, the reconciliation of installment highlights inside WhatsApp presents the two open doors and difficulties for emerging countries. While advanced installments can improve monetary incorporation and comfort, they additionally bring up issues about security, administrative structures, and the expected centralization of monetary power inside the application. These difficulties require a sensitive harmony among development and guaranteeing the security of clients in locales with different financial circumstances.

WhatsApp's effect stretches out past private correspondence and business communications; it has turned into a stage for urban commitment and social preparation in emerging countries. From political missions to local area drives, WhatsApp bunches have turned into an amazing asset for coordinating and dispersing data. This metro aspect of WhatsApp mirrors its ability to adjust to the different requirements of clients and networks, adding to social availability and support.

The instructive area in non-industrial countries has additionally encountered the extraordinary impact of WhatsApp. In regions where conventional methods of schooling face infrastructural challenges, the application has been used for distance learning, educator understudy correspondence, and the sharing of instructive assets. This variation features the application's flexibility in tending to different necessities inside advancing financial scenes.

WhatsApp's effect on correspondence patterns in agricultural countries has suggestions for social and monetary turn of events. The application plays had an impact in crossing over correspondence holes, encouraging financial strengthening, and empowering community commitment. Nonetheless, understanding the maximum capacity of WhatsApp's effect requires tending to the difficulties it presents, for example, protection concerns, deception, and the evenhanded combination of monetary elements.

As WhatsApp's prominence keeps on filling in agricultural countries, it highlights the requirement for smart approaches and procedures to tackle its advantages while relieving likely dangers. The stage's versatility, cost-viability, and arrangement with socio-social elements position it as a strong power forming correspondence patterns in the advancing scenes of emerging countries. The continuous development of WhatsApp and its reconciliation into different features of life in these locales signal a change in perspective in how people, organizations, and networks interface and impart in the computerized age.

Chapter 9

The Future of WhatsApp's Global Domination

Not long from now, WhatsApp remains at the front of worldwide correspondence, its scope reaching out a long ways past what its pioneers might have imagined in the beginning of its commencement. As innovation proceeds with its tireless walk forward, the scene of informing stages develops couple, and WhatsApp finds itself a player as well as a dominator in this steadily growing field.

One of the urgent variables adding to WhatsApp's worldwide mastery lies in its versatility. The stage has consistently embraced and coordinated arising advances, from computerized reasoning to expanded reality, making a vivid and dynamic client experience. The once-straightforward informing application has transformed into a multi-layered correspondence center point, obliging different necessities and inclinations.

As we dive into the fate of WhatsApp, the idea of a bound together correspondence stage becomes the dominant focal point. WhatsApp turns out to be something other than an informing application; it changes into a focal center point for a bunch of correspondence channels. Clients can flawlessly change from text-based discussions to superior quality video calls, direct conferences, and offer mixed media content without exchanging between various applications. This combination of correspondence channels improves client comfort as well as sets WhatsApp's situation as the go-to stage for complete, incorporated correspondence.

The development of WhatsApp rises above simple text and voice correspondence. The reconciliation of increased reality (AR) and computer generated reality (VR) innovations launches the stage into another aspect. Envision an existence where clients can share their environmental factors continuously through AR-improved video calls, carrying a feeling of actual presence to virtual collaborations. WhatsApp turns into a passage to shared encounters, overcoming any issues among physical and computerized domains.

Security, a perpetual worry in the computerized age, becomes the overwhelming focus later on cycles of WhatsApp. The stage pioneers progressed encryption conventions, guaranteeing start to finish security for a wide range of correspondence. Clients can take part in discussions with the certainty that their messages, calls, and shared content stay classified and secure. This obligation to protection not just satisfies the developing needs of an undeniably security-cognizant client base yet additionally fills in as a vital differentiator in the cutthroat scene of informing applications.

The fate of WhatsApp reaches out past private correspondence to rethink how organizations associate with their crowds. The stage develops into a hearty business specialized instrument, offering a set-up of highlights customized for undertakings. From client service chatbots controlled by man-made reasoning to get record sharing for cooperative activities, WhatsApp turns into a vital device for present day organizations hoping to smooth out their correspondence work processes.

As the lines between virtual entertainment and informing applications obscure, WhatsApp coordinates social elements that cultivate local area commitment. Clients can join interest-based gatherings, go to virtual occasions, and find new associations inside the stage. WhatsApp changes into a social environment, where people, organizations, and networks meet, cultivating a feeling of having a place and inter-connectedness.

The worldwide idea of WhatsApp's predominance turns out to be much more articulated as language obstructions disintegrate. High level language interpretation highlights, driven by AI calculations, empower clients from assorted etymological foundations to easily impart. This inclusivity expands WhatsApp's client base as well as cultivates a genuinely worldwide local area where social and phonetic contrasts become open doors for association as opposed to boundaries.

Later on, WhatsApp's effect reaches out past individual clients to impact cultural and political scenes. The stage turns into an impetus for city commitment, giving a space to informed conversations, grassroots developments, and the trading of thoughts. WhatsApp arises as an amazing asset for social change, empowering clients to coordinate, prepare, and advocate for purposes that make a difference to them.

The multiplication of Web of Things (IoT) gadgets further entwines with WhatsApp's development. Brilliant homes, associated vehicles, and wearable gadgets consistently coordinate with the stage, permitting clients to control and screen their environmental elements through instinctive WhatsApp interfaces. The limit between the advanced and actual domains proceeds to obscure, and WhatsApp sits at the nexus of this interconnected future.

Adaptation systems go through a change in outlook in store for WhatsApp. While the center informing highlights stay free for clients, the stage presents premium administrations and membership models for cutting edge highlights. Organizations influence WhatsApp's broad client base for designated promoting and supported con-tent, making a practical income stream without compromising the client experience.

Man-made consciousness turns into the foundation of WhatsApp's usefulness. Progressed chatbots controlled by normal language handling empower more modern associations, from customized client assistance to virtual friendship. The stage expects client needs, computerizing routine errands and giving a degree of comfort that becomes crucial in clients' day to day routines.

The idea of the metaverse flourishes in WhatsApp's development, rising above customary thoughts of online correspondence. Clients explore a computerized scene where virtual and actual real factors join flawlessly. WhatsApp turns into a passage to this metaverse, offering a stage for clients to convey as well as submerge themselves in a common computerized insight.

Schooling turns into a point of convergence coming down the line for WhatsApp. The stage teams up with instructive organizations to establish a virtual learning climate, where understudies and educators participate progressively conversations, share assets, and team up on projects. WhatsApp's instinctive point of interaction works with a smooth progress from conventional study halls to the computerized domain, democratizing admittance to schooling on a worldwide scale.

Medical care likewise encounters an upheaval through WhatsApp's coordination of telemedicine administrations. Clients can counsel medical care experts, share clinical records safely, and get customized wellbeing proposals inside the stage. WhatsApp turns into a virtual medical care center, rising above geological obstructions and expanding openness to clinical benefits.

The fate of WhatsApp isn't without challenges. As the stage grows its abilities, worries about information security and protection heighten. Finding some kind of harmony among advancement and shielding client data becomes fundamental. WhatsApp faces examination from administrative bodies, inciting the requirement for straightforward approaches and proactive measures to address likely dangers.

Rivals in the informing application field heighten their endeavors to oust WhatsApp from its worldwide platform. New contestants influence arising innovations and one of a kind elements to cut out their specialties, representing a steady danger to WhatsApp's strength. The stage answers with readiness, constantly advancing and remaining on the ball to keep up with its status as the favored decision for clients around the world.

9.1 Speculations on future developments and innovations

As we peer into the fogs representing things to come, the scene of innovative improvement seems both promising and confounding. Hypotheses flourish in regards to the direction of developments that might shape our reality in the years to come. From headways in man-made consciousness (computer based intelligence) to forward leaps in medical care and natural supportability, what's in store guarantees an embroidery of potential outcomes that could rethink the manner in which we live, work, and communicate.

One of the premier fields of hypothesis spins around the development of man-made reasoning. As figuring power keeps on flooding, the capacities of simulated intelligence are supposed to arrive at new levels. AI calculations, driven by huge datasets and refined brain organizations, are ready to upset the tech business as well as different features of our day to day routines. The possibility of computer based intelligence turning out to be more skilled at complex critical thinking, inventive assignments, and, surprisingly, the ability to appreciate anyone on a deeper level brings up issues about its mix into different fields.

In medical care, the crossing point of simulated intelligence and customized medication holds extraordinary commitment. Hypotheses recommend that man-made intelligence calculations will investigate individual hereditary profiles, empowering the customization of treatment plans in light of an individual's extraordinary hereditary cosmetics. This fitted way to deal with medical services could prompt more powerful therapies with less incidental effects, denoting a change in outlook from the conventional one-size-fits-all model. Also, artificial intelligence fueled indicative apparatuses may upgrade early location of illnesses, working on by and large visualization and decreasing medical care costs.

The domain of expanded reality (AR) and computer generated reality (VR) welcomes a plenty of hypotheses in regards to their combination into our day to day routines. The advancement of AR and VR innovations is expected to reclassify how we see and cooperate with the world. From vivid virtual encounters that mix consistently with our actual environmental factors to AR-improved route and data overlays, these advancements hold the possibility to reshape enterprises like gaming, instruction, and, surprisingly, proficient preparation.

As we mull over the future, the thought of the metaverse poses a potential threat not too far off. Theories flourish about a common virtual space where people can connect progressively, rising above geological limits. The metaverse is imagined as an intermingling of increased reality, computer generated reality, and the web, making an advanced domain where social connections, trade, and diversion flawlessly coincide. The ramifications of a completely acknowledged metaverse reach out past entertainment, offering new roads for coordinated effort, instruction, and, surprisingly, remote work.

Energy and ecological manageability are foremost worries as we imagine what's to come. Theories recommend a shift towards sustainable power sources on a worldwide scale, with headways in sunlight based, wind, and other green advances taking significant steps. The reconciliation of savvy matrices and energy stockpiling arrangements is expected to upgrade the productivity and dependability of environmentally friendly power frameworks, making ready for a more practical and ecologically cognizant energy scene.

The appearance of quantum registering presents a component of both fervor and vulnerability into the fate of innovation. Hypotheses about the groundbreaking force of quantum PCs in tackling complex issues, from cryptography to sedate revelation, flourish. The possibility to perform calculations at speeds recently considered unimaginable opens new wildernesses in logical examination and computational abilities. Notwithstanding, the difficulties related with keeping up with the soundness of quantum frameworks and tending to moral worries in regards to quantum registering's possible effect on encryption and security additionally fuel speculative conversations.

Blockchain and decentralized advancements keep on being subjects of extreme theory. The possible uses of blockchain reach out a long ways past digital forms of money, with hypotheses about its job in upsetting ventures, for example, finance, production network the board, and even administration. The idea of decentralized independent associations (DAOs), controlled by blockchain, flashes conversations about new models of administration that focus on straightforwardness, trust, and inclusivity.

Biotechnology remains at the bleeding edge of hypothesis in regards to forward leaps in medical services, horticulture, and then some. Headways in quality altering advances, for example, CRISPR, brief conversations about the possibility to kill hereditary illnesses and upgrade human capacities. Hypotheses additionally spin around the utilization of biotechnology in farming to foster harvests with further developed yields, protection from bothers, and more noteworthy dietary benefit, tending to worldwide food security challenges.

The fate of transportation fills extreme hypothesis about the development of electric and independent vehicles. As battery innovation improves and charging framework grows, electric vehicles (EVs) are expected to turn out to be more open and standard. The possibility of completely independent vehicles exploring our streets brings up issues about wellbeing, administrative structures, and the effect on customary businesses like transportation and operations.

Space investigation and colonization catch the aggregate creative mind, with hypotheses going from the achievability of human settlement on Mars to the digging of space rocks for valuable assets. Confidential space organizations, energized by enterprising visionaries, add to the story of a future where space travel isn't simply the domain of countries yet additionally a domain open to business adventures and human investigation.

The Web of Things (IoT) keeps on meshing itself into the texture of our regular routines, and hypotheses about its future ramifications are bountiful. A reality where interconnected gadgets impart consistently, upgrading processes and improving comfort, is not too far off. From savvy homes that expect inhabitants' requirements to modern applications that smooth out assembling processes, the IoT is ready to catalyze another time of availability and productivity.

Moral contemplations pose a potential threat in speculative conversations about the fate of innovation. As developments progress at a quick speed, inquiries regarding information protection, algorithmic predisposition, and the dependable improvement of arising innovations become progressively noticeable. Hypotheses rotate around the foundation of moral structures and guidelines to guarantee that innovative headways are lined up with cultural qualities and don't incidentally propagate imbalances.

Instruction remains at the nexus of hypothesis in regards to the reconciliation of innovation into learning conditions. The future might observer a shift towards customized, innovation driven instruction, with versatile learning stages, virtual homerooms, and man-made intelligence helped coaching becoming ordinary. Hypotheses likewise base on the democratization of training, as innovation opens new roads for mastering and ability advancement, rising above geological and financial boundaries.

As we explore the scene of future turns of events and advancements, cultural contemplations come to the very front. Hypotheses about the effect of innovative headways on business, disparity, and the actual texture of human connections shape conversations about the sort of world we are altogether endeavoring to construct. The requirement for mindful development, directed by moral standards and a pledge to the benefit of all, turns into a repetitive subject in speculative exchanges about what's to come.

All in all, what's to come stays a material whereupon our aggregate creative mind paints a horde of potential outcomes. From the reconciliation of cutting edge innovations in medical services, training, and transportation to the moral contemplations that go with these headways, the speculative scene is rich with possible directions. As we set out on this excursion into the obscure, the exchange of development, morals, and cultural qualities will shape the unfurling story of our mechanical future.

9.2 Potential challenges and opportunities for growth

Exploring the steadily developing scene of innovative headways presents a polarity of difficulties and potential open doors that length different areas of society. From the domains of business and advancement to the more extensive range of worldwide administration, the potential for both development and snags poses a potential threat. Understanding and tending to these difficulties while profiting by valuable open doors is vital for cultivating a feasible and comprehensive future.

One of the essential difficulties that organizations face in this quickly changing mechanical scene is the requirement for steady transformation. The speed of development, driven by forward leaps in man-made consciousness, computerization, and other extraordinary advances, requests a degree of readiness and adaptability that not all associations are ready to embrace.

Heritage frameworks, dug in work processes, and protection from change inside hierarchical societies can block the consistent coordination of new advancements, representing a critical obstacle for organizations planning to remain cutthroat.

In any case, inside these difficulties lies a variety of chances for development. Organizations that proactively embrace computerized change stand to acquire an upper hand. The coordination of cutting edge innovations, for example, distributed computing, information examination, and man-made reasoning, can smooth out tasks, improve efficiency, and give significant experiences to informed navigation. Organizations that explore this shift successfully position themselves for endurance as well as for supported development in the unique advanced scene.

Another test that arises right after mechanical progressions is the extending hole in advanced proficiency and access. While innovation vows to interface individuals and enable them with data, there is a gamble of abandoning specific sections of the populace. Financial differences, deficient schooling systems, and absence of admittance to computerized foundation can intensify disparities, making an advanced gap that hampers the comprehensive advantages of mechanical advancement.

In any case, tending to these difficulties presents a chance for cultural development and value. States, organizations, and instructive foundations can team up to connect the advanced gap through drives that advance computerized proficiency, put resources into innovation framework in underserved regions, and guarantee equivalent admittance to instructive assets. By effectively attempting to remember all sections of society for the computerized upset, we relieve the dangers of prohibition as well as open the maximum capacity of a mechanically engaged worldwide local area.

The moral contemplations encompassing arising advancements present the two difficulties and open doors. As man-made brainpower turns out to be more coordinated into day to day existence, inquiries concerning protection, algorithmic predisposition, and the capable utilization of information become progressively squeezing. Guaranteeing that mechanical headways line up with moral standards and cultural qualities requires a proactive methodology from both policymakers and industry pioneers.

However, inside these moral moves lies the valuable chance to shape a future where innovation serves the benefit of all. Laying out vigorous moral systems, straightforward administration designs, and industry principles can direct the turn of events and organization of innovations in a dependable way. Organizations that focus on moral contemplations construct entrust with their client base as well as add to the formation of a mechanical scene that focuses on human government assistance and regards individual freedoms.

Ecological maintainability is a test that poses a potential threat not too far off, especially as the interest for innovation keeps on developing. The creation and removal of electronic gadgets, energy utilization related with server farms, and the natural effect of digging assets for innovation parts all add to a critical biological impression.

In any case, the basic to address ecological worries presents a chance for development and economical practices. The improvement of eco-accommodating innovations, round economy models that advance reusing and reuse, and the reception of energy-effective practices in the tech business can make ready for a more supportable future. Organizations that proactively consolidate ecologically capable practices add to worldwide manageability objectives as well as position themselves as pioneers in corporate social obligation.

The steadily growing computerized domain delivers network protection challenges that request consistent cautiousness. As innovation turns out to be more basic to day to day existence, the dangers related with digital dangers, information breaks, and pernicious exercises raise. The interconnected idea of advanced frameworks enhances the expected effect of digital assaults, presenting dangers to individual protection, public safety, and the uprightness of basic foundation.

In any case, the test of online protection additionally presents open doors for advancement and development. The improvement of hearty network safety measures, encryption innovations, and high level danger location frameworks can strengthen advanced environments against possible dangers. Organizations having some expertise in online protection administrations wind up popular, offering arrangements that defend people, organizations, and legislatures from the advancing scene of digital dangers.

Worldwide administration faces a test in staying up with the quick progressions in innovation. The borderless idea of the computerized world frequently dominates customary administrative systems, making holes in oversight and responsibility. Issues, for example, cross-line information streams, computerized tax collection, and the moral utilization of arising advancements require global participation and administrative structures that rise above public limits.

Notwithstanding, the difficulties in worldwide administration additionally present a chance for cooperative arrangements. The improvement of worldwide guidelines, arrangements, and cooperative drives can encourage a blended way to deal with worldwide difficulties presented by innovation. Gatherings for strategic exchange, worked with by worldwide associations, can give a stage to countries to address shared concerns and work towards laying out a firm system for the mindful utilization of innovation on a worldwide scale.

The fate of work is going through a change in outlook with the reconciliation of computerization and man-made brainpower. While these advances offer expanded proficiency and efficiency, they likewise present difficulties as far as occupation removal and the requirement for upskilling the labor force to adjust to the changing requests of the computerized economy.

Notwithstanding, the development of work likewise presents amazing open doors for advancement and imagination. The mechanization of routine errands opens up HR to zero in on complex critical thinking, imagination, and jobs that require the ability to appreciate anyone on a deeper level. Drives that focus on reskilling and upskilling projects can engage the labor force to flourish in an innovation driven scene, guaranteeing that the advantages of robotization are shared impartially.

The medical care area wrestles with difficulties and valuable open doors in the midst of the combination of innovation. Electronic wellbeing records, telemedicine, and wearable wellbeing advances offer additional opportunities for proficient medical care conveyance, remote checking, and customized therapy plans. Nonetheless, worries about information security, the moral utilization of clinical information, and the evenhanded admittance to medical services innovations present huge difficulties.

However, inside the medical services scene, amazing open doors flourish for progressions that work on quiet results and smooth out medical care conveyance.

The reconciliation of man-made consciousness in diagnostics, the improvement of accuracy medication in light of individual hereditary profiles, and the utilization of innovation for preventive medical services measures address extraordinary open doors. Finding some kind of harmony among advancement and moral contemplations is vital in understanding the maximum capacity of innovation in medical care.

The crossing point of innovation and schooling presents the two difficulties and open doors for the fate of learning. The digitization of training, web based learning stages, and the utilization of computerized reasoning in versatile learning frameworks offer open doors for a more customized and open schooling. Notwithstanding, worries about the computerized partition, the nature of online instruction, and the requirement for successful educator preparing present difficulties that require insightful arrangements.

However, inside the instructive scene, the potential for development is enormous. Computer generated reality and expanded reality advances can make vivid growth opportunities, and information investigation can give experiences to fit instructive ways to deal with individual requirements. The fate of schooling lies in bridling innovation to make comprehensive, drawing in, and powerful learning conditions that get ready understudies for the difficulties of a quickly developing world.

All in all, what's in store is a perplexing embroidery of difficulties and valuable open doors that unfurl across different spaces. Exploring this scene requires an aggregate and proactive methodology from people, organizations, legislatures, and worldwide establishments. While difficulties like advanced imbalance, online protection dangers, and moral contemplations present huge obstacles, they additionally present open doors for development, manageable practices, and comprehensive development. Embracing the potential for positive change requires a pledge to capable turn of events, moral administration, and cooperative endeavors that rise above customary limits. In doing as such, we can on the whole shape a future where innovation fills in as a power for good, cultivating progress that isn't just mechanically progressed yet additionally socially and ecologically cognizant.

9.3 WhatsApp's role in shaping the future of global digital communication

WhatsApp, since its commencement, plays had a vital impact in molding the scene of worldwide computerized correspondence. As an informing stage that rises above borders and interfaces people across the world, WhatsApp has worked with individual discussions as well as turned into a necessary piece of business correspondence, cultural communications, and, surprisingly, political talk. Looking at the direction of WhatsApp's impact reveals a complex effect on the eventual fate of worldwide computerized correspondence.

At the center of WhatsApp's importance lies its easy to use interface and the straightforwardness of its informing highlights. From its initial days, WhatsApp situated itself as an open and instinctive stage for text informing. This effortlessness engaged an expansive client base, going from educated people to those less acquainted with cutting edge computerized instruments. As WhatsApp develops, this obligation to easy to understand configuration stays a foundation, guaranteeing that people from different foundations can consistently impart and share data.

The worldwide reach of WhatsApp has been a main impetus in its job as an impetus for culturally diverse correspondence. The stage separates language boundaries through highlights like moment interpretation, empowering clients who communicate in various dialects to participate in significant discussions. This inclusivity encourages a feeling of interconnectedness, where people from different regions of the planet can share encounters, thoughts, and viewpoints easily. In forming the fate of worldwide correspondence, WhatsApp remains as an image of solidarity in variety.

The advancement of WhatsApp reaches out past conventional text informing. The stage's mix of interactive media highlights, for example, photograph and video sharing, has changed how clients impart and share encounters. Later on, this pattern is probably going to escalate, with more extravagant sight and sound substance turning into a staple in computerized discussions. The visual and intelligent nature of mixed media informing improves the general correspondence experience, making it more vivid and locking in.

Besides, the ascent of voice informing and great video approaches WhatsApp has re-imagined continuous correspondence. As innovation propels, what's in store holds the commitment of much more modern general media connections. Expanded reality (AR) and computer generated reality (VR) advancements might track down their direction into WhatsApp, making a virtual space where clients can share encounters progressively, rising above the constraints of actual distance. This potential development mirrors a more extensive pattern in the computerized correspondence scene, where stages constantly endeavor to make cooperations more similar and dynamic.

WhatsApp's part in business correspondence has been consistently extending, denoting a critical change in how endeavors draw in with their clients and partners. The presentation of WhatsApp Business, with highlights like business profiles, robotized reactions, and value-based capacities, positions the stage as a flexible device for client relations and promoting. Later on, WhatsApp is probably going to additionally set its spot in the business biological system, with additional organizations utilizing the stage for client assistance, item dispatches, and designated advertising efforts.

The eventual fate of WhatsApp as a business specialized device likewise converges with the domain of computerized reasoning (man-made intelligence). Hypotheses flourish in regards to the mix of computer based intelligence controlled chatbots that can deal with client questions, give customized suggestions, and smooth out business processes. This blend of man-made intelligence and business correspondence on WhatsApp holds the possibility to reform how organizations collaborate with their crowds, offering a degree of proficiency and personalization that was once uncommon.

Protection has arisen as a focal worry in the computerized age, and WhatsApp has answered by carrying out powerful safety efforts. The stage's obligation to start to finish encryption guarantees that client messages, calls, and shared content stay private and secure. As advanced correspondence turns out to be more imbued in day to day existence, the interest for protection is probably going to heighten. WhatsApp's enduring obligation to client security positions it as a confided in stage in a period where information assurance is fundamental.

While protection stays serious areas of strength for a for WhatsApp, the stage has not been safe to contentions and discussions encompassing falsehood and phony news. The sending highlight, which permits clients to handily impart messages to various contacts, has now and again worked with the quick spread of unsubstantiated data. WhatsApp has done whatever it may take to resolve this issue by restricting the sending of messages and carrying out elements to recognize sent content. The continuous test lies in finding some kind of harmony between safeguarding security and forestalling the abuse of the stage for the spread of bogus data.

In the political circle, WhatsApp has arisen as a strong device for data scattering, political crusading, and grassroots preparation. Political pioneers and gatherings influence the stage to associate with citizens, share their plans, and coordinate assemblies. The stage's capacity to contact a monstrous crowd progressively has changed the elements of political correspondence, making it more straightforward, quick, and open. As the political scene keeps on developing, WhatsApp is probably going to assume an undeniably noticeable part in forming general assessment and impacting political talk.

The fate of WhatsApp interweaves with the more extensive idea of the metaverse, where computerized and actual real factors unite. While WhatsApp right now works in the domain of message, voice, and video correspondence, the metaverse presents open doors for a more vivid and interconnected insight. Virtual gatherings, shared virtual spaces, and cooperative exercises could become necessary parts representing things to come WhatsApp experience. This development lines up with a more extensive pattern in computerized correspondence stages, which are investigating ways of making on the web communications more exact and coordinated with clients' actual environmental elements.

Language, a basic part of correspondence, is likewise liable to go through changes on WhatsApp. High level language interpretation highlights, driven by artificial intelligence and regular language handling, may turn out to be more modern. This could separate language obstructions considerably further, permitting clients to impart flawlessly with people who communicate in various dialects. The eventual fate of WhatsApp could see a more comprehensive and different worldwide local area, where etymological contrasts are explored easily, cultivating a feeling of interconnectedness.

Adaptation methodologies are expected to assume a critical part in WhatsApp's future. While the center informing highlights have customarily been free for clients, the stage has presented different adaptation drives. WhatsApp Business, for example, offers a scope of business instruments through a membership model. Later on, organizations might track down extra open doors for designated promoting, supported content, and premium highlights on the stage. Finding some kind of harmony among adaptation and client experience will be essential for WhatsApp to keep up with its allure and client base.

Man-made reasoning is probably going to penetrate further into the texture of WhatsApp's usefulness. Progressed chatbots, driven by normal language handling and AI, could upgrade the effectiveness of collaborations. These simulated intelligence fueled bots may deal with routine inquiries as well as give customized proposals, making the general client experience more helpful and custom-made to individual inclinations. As computer based intelligence innovation keeps on propelling, its incorporation into WhatsApp could rethink how clients draw in with the stage.

The development of WhatsApp's impact into regions, for example, instruction and medical services is additionally inside the domain of hypothesis. Joint efforts with instructive establishments could prompt virtual homerooms, where understudies and educators connect progressively, rising above topographical requirements. In medical care, WhatsApp might develop into a stage for telemedicine administrations, permitting clients to talk with medical services experts, share clinical records safely, and get customized wellbeing suggestions. These potential developments line up with the more extensive pattern of computerized stages becoming essential to different parts of day to day existence.

Challenges, be that as it may, persevere not too far off. As WhatsApp grows its abilities, worries about information security and protection increase. The stage's obligation to start to finish encryption is honorable, yet the developing scene of online protection requests consistent cautiousness. Finding some kind of harmony among development and protecting client data stays a foremost test, especially in a period where information breaks and security concerns rule titles.

Additionally, rivalry in the informing application field is wild, with new participants continually competing for focus and piece of the pie. Arising innovations and inventive elements from contenders represent a steady danger to WhatsApp's predominance. The stage should remain coordinated, ceaselessly improving and expecting client needs to keep up with its status as the favored decision for worldwide correspondence.

Administrative difficulties additionally pose a potential threat. State run administrations overall are wrestling with the guideline of advanced stages, especially in regions concerning security, information assurance, and falsehood. Exploring an intricate snare of guidelines while guaranteeing client protection and opportunity of articulation presents a continuous test for WhatsApp. A proactive way to deal with consistence, straightforward correspondence with administrative bodies, and cooperation on capable administration will be fundamental in tending to these difficulties.

Printed in the USA
CPSIA information can be obtained
at www.ICGtesting.com
LVHW051344211223
766878LV00074B/1348